May 12, 1985

To Carolyn,
    With our love and
support for your
continuing spiritual
journey.
            Grace + Peg

Guide Lectures for Self-Transformation

EVA PIERRAKOS

Cover and interior design:
Peter Ross, Ross Design
Associates, Inc.

Table of Contents

Introduction

In these fifteen lectures a spirit guide of marvellous wisdom and love shows a way of self-purification. They are a sampling of the 258 Guide lectures given through the channel of Eva Pierrakos from 1957 to her death in 1979.

This path leads home: to the reconnection with the higher self, God within. The lectures help us to recognize the obstacles that stand between our outer self and our inner truth and teach us how to overcome them. The obstacles are in our own lower nature, self-created and therefore removable. Finding the causes of the existence of this lower nature, understanding ourselves in the light of truth, love, and wisdom, makes self-transformation possible and releases the power of positive creation. The unique contribution of these lectures to every human endeavor of self-transcendence lies in that they open our eyes to a consciousness through which life itself becomes the path, the teacher. Every lecture can be applied in a very practical way to one's daily experience. Revolutionary concepts bring together psychological work of the deepest kind with cosmic spiritual and metaphysical wisdom.

When I read my first Guide lecture, I felt as if suddenly a light had burst open within me: it brought a great joy of understanding and hope to my soul and I knew I had found my long-sought path. Beyond psychology, beyond conventional religion, it points the way towards the union of the created with the Creator.

Eva was born in 1915 in Vienna, the daughter of the well-known Austrian novelist Jakob Wasserman. Her mediumship began to manifest at first in the form of automatic writing. She pursued the development of her mediumship with great devotion and perseverance, following the guidance received through her channel. Eva always referred to the entity manifesting through her as "the Guide" and to her ability to give spiritual guidance and to help people in their self-development as her life task.

Eva (then Eva Broch) came to the United States in 1939 and continued her work in New York, giving Guide sessions and an ongoing series of trance lectures to those who were guided to her. She was a beautiful, vibrantly alive woman with a keen intelligence who enjoyed life in all its aspects. She loved people and animals and enjoyed skiing, swimming, and dancing. In 1971 she married psychiatrist John C. Pierrakos, one of the founders of bioenergetics and later, core energetics. The energetic work became an essential part of the pathwork and contributed to its expansion. Together, with the help of a small group of enthusiastic "pathworkers," they founded the first pathwork center in a secluded valley in the Catskill Mountains near Phoenicia, New York in 1972. It was incorporated as a non-profit educational institution under the name Center for the Living Force. Now called the Phoenicia Pathwork Center, it continues as a focal point for individual and community pathwork.

In spite of the fact that, until now, the Guide lectures have only been available individually as transcribed from Eva's tapes, hundreds, or perhaps thousands, of people from all over the world have already found their way to this particular spiritual path. The time has come to publish the lectures in book form, and the process of preparing the entire series for publication has begun. Meanwhile, enjoy this introductory volume—read it with an open mind and open heart. Be guided and nourished.

Judith Saly
for the Publication Committee

Phoenicia Pathwork Center, January 1984

Note and Acknowledgment

We have chosen these particular lectures as a representative selection from the wide spectrum of the Guide's teachings. Since in this volume we are not printing them in their original sequence, the occasional references to previous lectures should be disregarded. You can find all the lectures listed in their original order at the end of the book.

Eva delivered her lectures in a state of trance, sitting on a straight-backed chair, with eyes closed. The lectures were always tape-recorded and afterwards Eva transcribed them herself. For this volume, we did only a minimal copy-editing, so as to preserve their original flavor. Also, though the generic use of "man," and "he," is becoming less and less acceptable, we decided not to tamper with the text in this respect, so as to avoid clumsiness or the temptation to rewrite entire sentences.

The Guide uses certain expressions, such as "images," in a very specific sense. You will find a short glossary of these terms printed after the lectures.

The publication of this book was the inspiration of Harold M. Wit and was made possible by his generous contribution.

The group whose love, effort, and guidance led to the form and format of this volume include Laurent Low, John Saly, Judith Saly, Adrienne Winogrand, Bert Shaw, Moira Shaw, Elizabeth Mylonas, Peter Schaffer, Judith Garten and Irving Warhaftig.

The Call

R E E T I N G S in the Name of the Lord. I
bring you His blessings, my friends.

There are very few people indeed who have
no belief in God at all. Almost everyone somehow
has at least a feeble belief in a Higher Intelligence,
in a Superior Wisdom that created this universe.
Yet there are few people who know how to continue on consequentially from
this thought. They limit God all the time.

There are many of you who admit God exists; God and this Higher
Intelligence—or whatever you choose to call it—are of course one and the
same. Yet you do not believe that it could be possible in this wonderful
creation that an entity of higher intelligence than human beings should find
it possible, if certain conditions are met, to manifest to you through a human instrument. This, you think, is incredible. This is something you cannot believe. But why, my friends? Why is it so hard to believe? It is certainly
not incredible that there should exist creatures of higher intelligence, of
greater wisdom, endowed with more love than human beings! There should
then be the possibility of communication with them.

A hundred years ago it would have seemed impossible to you that a
machine could fly in the sky, or that you could turn a knob and hear music
which is played hundreds of miles away, or that you could turn a knob and
see pictures. Often, because some people whom you trust declare that something is possible and scientific, you agree that it is so even though you yourself never experienced it. Why then, when communication with the spirit
world of God is manifested to you, do you still say somewhere in your mind

that it is impossible, that it must be, if not a trick, a delusion, then the subconscious of the medium or something of the sort. Is that really reasonable, my friends? If so many other astounding things are possible in this world of yours, why should it not be equally possible that God sends you His emissaries of truth for your benefit? This, in itself, is not more astounding than so many other things that you have freely accepted.

Furthermore, there are a number of people who know and admit that communication with the beyond is possible. They have experienced it; they have no possible doubt about it. Yet they deny the possibility of such communication with higher entities than themselves. This is even more unreasonable! Although it is quite true that a communication with divine spirits is infinitely more difficult to obtain, which is as it should be, it is highly illogical to think that it is impossible. If God has created any possibility of communication with people on the other side, then He must also have given you the means of communing with higher spheres where you can receive teachings that further you spiritually and bring you nearer to God.

So, my friends, communication with divine spheres is possible; it has always been possible, and it will always be possible. How frequently it occurs depends solely on man, on whether he meets the necessary requirements. I have occasionally mentioned what these requirements are and I may mention them again in the future, but they are too lengthy for me to go over now. However, any of you who are seriously interested can find out about the mechanics of this and also what is necessary to obtain communication with divine spheres; what the difference is between such advisable communication and that with earthbound and erring spirits. In fact, any of you who really want to judge have the duty to do so; otherwise you have no right to say, even to yourself, that it is impossible.

There are many people who are called! God is calling them. A person's spiritual development determines whether this call will come forth. Granted, there are many, many people living on earth who have not experienced such a call. They are still in spiritual childhood and such a call would be meaningless to them. They have not yet attained the strength and development necessary to follow it; therefore, God waits until they have reached the necessary maturity in the course of various incarnations in which they gather experience and wisdom and, step-by-step develop spiritually. But at some time this call must come forth, and I venture to say that everyone of you sitting in this room has been called.

How do you feel this call, you might ask. As I have said repeatedly, man consists of two natures: the higher and the lower self which are in conflict with one another. The higher self registers this call and pushes the person in a certain direction which the conscious self cannot immediately interpret. The conscious self just feels a certain longing, a certain dissatisfaction with the present life, even when you carry out all your earthly duties to the best of your ability. Nonetheless, there is a certain voice within you, a certain pressure; it seems as though you are being pushed in some direction and you do not know quite where as yet. But you will find out, provided you do not fight against it and do not give in to your lower self.

In the first place, you do not know where, why, or what it all means. If your lower self were not also alive within you, it would be comparatively easy to follow the call. But your lower self does not want to make any effort, it does not want any change, and it holds you back and furnishes you with many excuses not to follow your higher self. The excuses are manifold: "There is no time." They take the form of doubts and so on and so forth. These are all rationalizations. You, who are inexperienced in differentiating and pulling off your masks, pretexts, and self-illusions, believe the voice of your lower self because you want to believe these rationalizations; it is so much easier. But until this fight is successfully over with, once and for all, you will not have peace—never, my friends! The call will become stronger and stronger as you go on, and the more you resist it, the more dissatisfied you must become with your life. The more God can expect from you because of your basic spiritual development, the more dissatisfied you must be if you do not follow this call.

Mankind has asked time and time again why there are so many people who are inferior to others and who are nonetheless much happier. This appears to be an injustice. Why is this so? Less can be expected of a child in a lower grade than of a child in a higher grade. If you do not perform according to your development, you must be dissatisfied with your outer life as well as with your inner life.

Now that you have understood how the call is felt, I will explain to you what follows it and what is expected of you. Your lower self has some idea of it. If it had not, it would not fight against it. Now what does God want from you when He calls you? He does not expect you to be a martyr or to fulfill tremendous tasks; though he may expect the latter of some of you, he does not expect it from most of you. You can fulfill His wishes between your four walls and no one has to know about it. Who is to say what is a big task and what is a little one? Simply because you are famous and in the limelight does not necessarily mean that your task is a bigger one than if you work spiritually in solitude and no one knows about it. What God wants from each and every one of you, as the first step and necessary preliminary before you can give to others, is self-development, self-purification, and self-knowledge. This is the tearing off of your masks; the tearing away of all your delusions concerning yourself and your inner or outer motives. God expects this from you.

Whoever is not quite happy and harmonious can answer himself this way: "I have not quite followed God's call." Only you yourself will thus be able to answer any questions about this. How happy are you? How well-balanced are you? How harmonious are you "inside"? This question does not necessarily apply to outside conditions, for outside you may have troubles, but if you are truly on the right path and fulfill God's will for you, no matter what your outer difficulties may or may not be, you must be happy. That should be your yardstick and confirmation of where you stand and how much of your task you are fulfilling, my friends. I want each one of you, when you go home tonight, to think about the following: "How happy am I? How satisfied am I with my life and with myself?" If there is any disharmony or any dissatisfaction, you will then know the answer.

If you really want to follow the call, you can! Do not say, "I do not know how or where to turn; I cannot do it alone." Of course, you cannot do it alone. First you must really want to do it, first you must decide clearly and unconditionally, then God will guide you wherever it may be and through whatever means may be best for you so that you receive the necessary help from outside, so that you can develop yourself within to the highest degree that can be expected of you.

It is not enough that you lead a decent life and are a so-called ethical person who does no harm to others and who does not violate earthly laws. This may be enough for a person who is a younger soul, but not for any of you, my friends. So give yourself the answer tonight and test yourself: "How much do I really want to follow the call, even if it means that I have to use will power, effort, patience—and, perhaps, suffer some pain.

Self-recognition and the tearing off of masks is always painful during the process, although it is a great relief afterwards. It is a relief that will bring a very new peace into your soul, once you have overcome the initial resistance. So you must realize that first you have to go to battle with your lower self; you have to enlist your conscious will power in order to be able to conquer your lower self. Combined with your higher self, your will-directing consciousness must win. But do not be superficial about it. Test yourself again and again as to how sincere, how deep is your desire to do God's will. How much are you willing to sacrifice? This sacrifice may be one of comfort, self-delusion, selfishness, of the holding on to your various faults and weaknesses. How much are you willing to give up of all this?

First this will appear to be a tremendous sacrifice on your part, but only while you are in battle. Afterwards will come the realization that you have freed yourself of the burdens and chains that were directly responsible for your unhappiness. Afterwards you will recognize without a shadow of a doubt that God's will for you is really no sacrifice, for it brings you happiness on every plane of existence: physically, mentally, emotionally, and spiritually. But as long as you have not actually won this victory, the decision and its consequences will appear to you to be a sacrifice—this is also what God wants. He does not give the realization of all this before, but only afterwards! In other words, until you have completely decided to do the will of God, whatever this may mean, and until you have made your lower self submissive—and this can be done if your will power penetrates into all layers of consciousness—you should not even try to think what you should do or what the practical consequences are concerning this decision of yours. What follows next will be made known to you through guidance, through inspiration. You do not have to worry about it now.

First, you have to prepare the ground, to lay the foundation through this initial fight within yourself to make the great decision. Only then can you cross the first threshold on the path to God. But this fight cannot be won in one day. It is sometimes a hard battle and when you go into it, you should know what you are letting yourself in for. However, I can promise you my friends, if you go about it in this way and have reached the stage when you can say, "I want it, one hundred percent," you have won the most important and the most difficult of all battles and nothing that follows on this path can be compared to it. You will emerge from this battle not only victorious, but also a great deal stronger than you were before; and also, needless to say, a somewhat happier person. You will not be quite the same person as you were before you entered this battle.

God will help you to take the next step and this you may safely believe. Ask God for the strength to win this battle. All you have to do is think of asking God for His help. Many people make wonderful prayers using beautiful and poetic words, but they seldom think of their immediate spiritual problems, and this is a great mistake, for there are also certain laws covering this issue. If you ask for help, you can receive it, particularly such help as I have mentioned to you. You are expected to turn to God with these difficulties. If you really want this help with all your heart and ask God for it, He will answer you. I can promise it. The only question remaining is how honestly do you really want to? How much is there still of your lower self which is powerful enough to pull you in the opposite direction ? As long as you do not face this and do not want to realize the significance of it, you cannot win, and your prayer will not have the desired effect because it is halfhearted and full of reservations. This is why I am giving you these words, so that you will know how to win your battle and follow your call. Only then will you find the peace and the harmony along with the fulfill-ment for which you are still longing—all of you.

Everyone knows that selfishness is wrong. By the same token, every-one knows that to give to your brothers and sisters is right. It is according to divine law, and it makes you happy to do so. Now, there are many dif-ferences in this giving. For many people the easiest way out, if I may say so, is to give financially. It hurts least and it means the smallest sacrifice. Everyone knows, on the other hand, that to give love is the greatest gift of all. And each one of you asks nothing better than to be able to give love. But how many of you find yourselves in the position to say, "If only I could, but how? I cannot, but I would like to do so. I am unable to love as much as I want to love." Oh yes, my dear ones, this means your soul is sick in some way and it must be cured. You cannot effect this cure alone, but God will help you. If all your inner currents were flowing according to divine law, you would certainly be able to love. Each one of your faults and short-comings is a direct hindrance to the unfolding of love. When I say unfold-ment, I mean that this love you wish to give forth is already within you. You cannot receive it from outside; it exists within you. It is only covered by certain layers that obstruct your love and prevent it from shining through, from manifesting itself. These layers are, as I said, your faults, your fears, and your ignorance of spiritual law. Therefore, these layers have to disappear, and this can only be accomplished by your very personal and serious endeavors. This is the path to God. This is what it means to follow the call.

Each one of your faults is a direct or indirect hindrance to love. You can never learn love through forcing yourself, but love will grow and evolve as a consequence when you purify yourself. One of the best meditations is to think about this: "What are my faults? And how could this fault possibly be a hindrance to the manifestation of the love that obviously must be hidden within me?" I challenge each one of you to present me with an example, for at the first instance you may think a number of your faults have absolutely no bearing on the unfoldment of love, and yet it is so.

At the same time, there is a wonderful and direct road, in addition to the indirect one just mentioned. Both should be taken simultaneously to further the growth of love within you. If you could bring yourself to learn what I will tell you now, you would gain a powerful weapon to cure yourself of many sick currents within your soul and you would unfold the love existing in you.

Each living individual has the understandable tendency to want to appear superior when he deals with his fellow creatures. He hides his faults, he hides his shortcomings and he wants to show his best side. Why? This is because he craves admiration, he craves acceptance, and he craves love. He thinks that showing his best side will bring him love. And yet you all know that if you want to receive love, you have to give it first. Do you really give love by impressing other people? In effect, this is what you actually believe consciously or subconsciously. On the other hand, you very decidedly give love in the deepest sense if you give and show yourself as you really are, without any masks—even if it means a little humiliation.

Yes, my friends, in this way you give the greatest gift. Why? This is because your fellow creatures feel just as unsure as you do. If to them you seem as perfect as you want to appear, their inferiority complexes will grow. They will think or feel, consciously or unconsciously: "He is so perfect—or she is so perfect—why can't I be that way?" They will feel even lonelier and more deflated and they will despise themselves even more. Therefore they will, in their blindness and as their only defense, put an even tighter shell around themselves. This separates them even more from their brothers and sisters and is similar to what you are doing by trying so hard to appear independent, hard, and oh so perfect! On the other hand, if you show yourself as you really are, with all your weaknesses and without any pretense, you make a great and generous gift; your brother or sister will say and feel, "Well, he is not any better than I am," and it will give him a lift. He will relax, will feel less lonely. Then do you know what will happen? You will receive in this way exactly what you have set out to gain: love, admiration.

You will receive love because you have first given up expecting it. You know the spiritual law which states that first you have to give up what you want to gain. You have given up admiration which means you have given up making an impression. You have given up expecting love from others because you appear to be so wonderful, and instead you have made a gift to others by diminishing their loneliness in their supposed imperfection. Each one thinks he is quite alone with his imperfections, even though he may see and criticize the imperfection of others all the time. This is one of the paradoxes of the blind and undeveloped self.

You have given up your vanity. You have given up some of your ego. This is why you must receive in this way, and in this way alone, what you never succeeded in receiving the old way, which your lower self chose in its blindness. If you give up yourself in this way, you bestow the greatest gift you can possibly give to another human being—therefore the law must take effect. It is such a simple way, my dear ones, so simple that none of you will ever think of it. And yet, at first it does not appear easy. It seems difficult to pull yourself down from that high place you consciously or subconsciously have built for yourself. Once you have taken this step in spite of all resistance, you must see divine law working within you and outside of you. This result must come.

Wherever there is a problem that you cannot solve, try this. Try it! You do not have to exaggerate; you do not have to go to strangers and pull yourself down. This might even be embarrassing for others if it is not done quite naturally and unostentatiously. Just take off your mask and be natural. Find out what and who you really are and be that person. Here, too, you will receive help, opportunity, and inspiration as to when and how to do it, if you once decide to do so and ask God for His help. All of a sudden, if you leave yourself open for it, you will find yourself in a position—perhaps with some member of your family or some friend—to discover for the first time in your life and become conscious of the fact that you have so far put on an act, that you have not given yourself as you really are. Once you become conscious of this, you will be able to act as you really are, my friends, and without any pretense.

No sickly exaggerations! No extremes! As in everything else, here too there exist two extremes. There are a number of people who indulge in self-contempt, pulling themselves down in the eyes of others. They say, "I am so bad, I am such a sinner, and I am this and I am that." This is as insincere a mask as the other extreme. Such a person wants by these means to accomplish the very same thing as the other group of people. This is quite smart, although this measure is often taken unconsciously. By accusing yourself, you take the weapon out of the hands of others. In this way, they find it quite impossible to accuse you and are even inclined to contradict your self-accusations, and thus the ego is bolstered. Furthermore, you often think that accusing yourself is quite sufficient; you do not have to do anything further in overcoming your shortcomings. This is just as bad as the other extreme.

If you think about these words, think of the two extremes. Whoever tends more to one of them will not find it so easy to slip into the opposite. It is important at the beginning only that you know your weakness and your tendency, for only what is truly genuine will have an effect. Of that you can be quite sure! This too is a law.

I will retire and leave you with the blessings of the Lord. Receive His love, for there is actually a great blessing in this room right now. If you are open to it, though perhaps not all of you can see this shining force, you may feel it and receive it and use it for God. Be in peace.

The God Image

G R E E T I N G S. I bring you blessings in the name of God. Blessed is this hour, my dearest friends.

In the Bible it is said that you should not create an image of God. Most people believe this statement means that you should not draw a picture or make a statue of God. But this is in no sense the entire meaning. If you think about this statement a little more profoundly, you will come to the conclusion that this could not be all that is implied in this commandment. With what you have learned so far on this path, you will now understand that this refers to the inner image. Most people are still so involved in their own wrong conclusions, in their irrational impressions that they are bound to have an image of God, as well as of other subjects. You are bound to have images of those subjects that are most important in your life.

At an early age the child experiences his first conflict with authority. Recently I talked at length about this. The child also learns that God is the highest authority. Therefore, it is not surprising that the child projects his own subjective experiences with authority onto his imaginings about God. Hence an image is formed, and whatever the child's and later the adult's attitude toward authority, his attitude toward God will most probably be colored and influenced by it.

A child experiences all kinds of authority. When the child is prohibited from doing what he enjoys most, he experiences authority as hostile. When parental authority grants favors to the child, allows him to indulge his desires, authority will be felt as benign. When there is a predominance of one kind of authority in childhood, that will be the unconscious attitude toward God. In many instances, however, children experience a mixture of both. Then the combination of these two kinds of authority will form their image of God. In the measure that a child experiences fear and frustration, in that measure will fear and frustration unconsciously be felt toward God. God is then felt to be a punishing, severe, and often even unfair and unjust force that one has to contend with. I know, my friends, that you do not think so consciously. In this work you are used to finding emotional reactions that do not at all correspond to your conscious concepts on whatever subject. The less the unconscious concept coincides with the conscious one, the greater is the shock when one realizes the discrepancy.

Practically everything the child enjoys most is forbidden. Whatever gives most pleasure is prohibited, usually for his own welfare; this the child cannot understand. It happens that parents also do this out of their own ignorance and fear. The child thus is impressed that everything most pleasurable in the world is subject to punishment from God, the highest and sternest authority.

In addition, you are bound to encounter human injustice in the course of your life, in childhood as well as in adulthood. Particularly if these injustices are perpetrated by people who stand for authority—and are therefore unconsciously associated with God—your unconscious belief in God's severe injustice is strengthened. Hence your fear of God is strengthened.

All this forms an image which makes, if properly analyzed, a monster out of God. This god, living in your unconscious mind, is really more of a Satan.

You yourself have to find out in this work how much of an image—or variations thereof—holds true for you personally. Is your soul impregnated with similar wrong concepts? If and when the realization of such an impression becomes conscious within a growing human being, it is often not understood that this concept of God is false and does not mean that God is actually the way in which He is experienced in the psyche. Then the person turns away from Him altogether and wants no part of the monster he has discovered hovering in his mind. This, by the way, is the true reason for most cases of atheism. The turning away is just as erroneous as the opposite extreme which consists of fearing a god who is severe, unjust, pious, self-righteous and cruel. He who unconsciously maintains the distorted God-image rightly fears Him and has to cajole Him for favors. Once again, you have a good example of two opposite extremes both of which lack truth to an equal extent.

Now let us examine the case wherein a child experiences benign authority to a greater extent than he experiences fear and frustration. Let us assume the child is spoiled and pampered. Doting parents fulfill every wish of the child, indulge his every whim. They do not instill a sense of responsibility in the child so that, in consequence, he can get away with practically everything. The God-image resulting from such a condition is, at first and superficial sight, closer to a true concept of God. He is forgiving, "good," loving, indulgent. This causes the personality to unconsciously think he can get away with anything in the eyes of his god. He thinks he can cheat life and avoid self-responsibility. To begin with, he will know much less fear. But since life cannot be cheated, one's own life-plan cannot be cheated, the results of his wrong attitude will be such that conflicts, and therefore fear, will be generated by a chain-reaction of wrong thinking, feeling and action. An inner confusion arises since life as it is in reality does not correspond to the unconscious God-image and concept.

Many sub-divisions of these two main categories exist in one soul, as well as many combinations of them. Depending upon the particular kind of predominant authority in childhood, the image is likely to be stronger in one direction, although even this cannot be generalized. It also depends on the characteristics that the entity has brought into this life, and the development in this particular respect achieved in former incarnations. The more that development has advanced in this area, the less are surroundings able to influence the psyche.

Apart from that, other factors play a role. It may well be that; for instance, hostile authority is the predominant factor. Let us say one parent is domineering and therefore the atmosphere in the child's home is filled with fear of this parent. The other parent may fit into the second category. Although this influence is outwardly weaker, it may create a much stronger impression on the soul and the image may be stronger in that direction. The same holds true in the opposite case. Although severity, injustice and fear may have been the weaker elements in manifestation during childhood, the impression on the individual soul may be much stronger and has therefore created a stronger image. But almost always, both currents can be found.

How, in what way, and why, what the attitude to the individual parent or parent-substitute was and is, all have to be found out and investigated in the image work. But do keep in mind, my friends, that both alternatives are to be looked for, even if one appears stronger to begin with. The pampering and indulgent God-image is not an additional factor to the monster-image, but often the very reaction to and compensation for it. The personality may grapple with these two false concepts unconsciously, but can never come out clear in this battle, because both concepts are false, while he unconsciously tries to find out which is right. In every child's life both kinds of authority are experienced, no matter how much more strongly one manifests. You may have one indulgent and one hard parent. Or you may even have two indulgent parents but a severe teacher who instills fear in you and has a greater influence on your inner growth than you realize, or the severe authority may be another relative or a sibling. One never is influenced by just one kind of authority.

It is very important, my friends, to find out what your God-image is. It is basic and determines all other attitudes, images and patterns, throughout life. Hence you should all examine this attitude which may be deeply hidden within yourself. Do not be deceived by your conscious convictions. Rather try to examine and analyze your emotional reactions to authority, to your parents, to your fears and expectancies. Out of that you will gradually discover what you feel about God rather than what you think. The whole scale between these two opposite poles is reflected in your God-image, from hopelessness and despair in the emotional conviction of an unjust universe to self-indulgence, rejection of self-responsibility, and the expectation of a god who pampers you.

Now the question of how to dissolve such an image arises. How do you dissolve any image? First you have to become fully conscious of the wrong concept. That is not as easily nor as quickly accomplished as it would seem, for you may be aware of it to some degree, yet you do not by any means recognize all its implications, effects and influences in your personality. You may not have recognized its significance on all levels of your being. This must always be the first step.

You may be aware of an image—which is always false, otherwise it would not be an image—but you may not even be aware that it is false. Even in your intellectual perception you are but partly convinced that the image-conclusion is incorrect. As long as this is so, you cannot free yourself of the enslaving chains of falsity. So the second step is to set your intellectual ideas straight.

It is needless to repeat that the proper formation of the intellectual concept should never be superimposed on the still lingering emotional false concept. This would only cause suppression. But, on the other hand, you should not allow the wrong conclusions and images, rising to the surface due to the work you have done so far, to make you believe that they are true. Sometimes you do fall into this error, in a subtle way. Realize that the so-far-suppressed concepts and ideas have to evolve clearly into consciousness; nurse the awareness of them in your surface-consciousness, but realize that they are false. In some instances the right concept is easy to formulate. Then these two should be compared. You should constantly check how much you still deviate emotionally from the right intellectual concept.

Check this discrepancy quietly, without inner haste or anger at yourself that your emotions do not follow your thinking as quickly as you would like. Give them time to grow. This is best accomplished by constant observation and comparison of the wrong and the right concept. Realize that your emotions need time to adjust, but do everything in your power to give them the opportunity to grow, which you can do through the process just described. Observe the emotions despite the resistances and the pretexts they can muster, for there is always that part in you that resists change and growth. This part in the human personality is very shrewd. Be wise to these ruses.

As I have said, some concepts are easy to formulate. They are obvious. To see this merely requires a little thinking through. The resisting emotions do not care whether the proper concept is obvious or not. In either case they will find ways and means of trying to avoid a change of inner attitude. As far as your intellectual understanding is concerned, you must differentiate between two kinds of concepts: those that are obvious if you think about them and those requiring development, inner enlightenment in order to formulate the proper concept even in your intellect.

Prayer for recognition is an important part. Observe in times of prayer how sincerely you desire the answer! This is important. You may dutifully pray for recognition, but inside there is a resisting block that can be felt if you set out to look for it. Then at least you know that not God but you yourself obstruct light and freedom. Then you can begin arguing with that part in yourself that persists in being childish and unreasonable.

As far as the proper concept about God is concerned, this is certainly one of the most difficult awarenesses to come by because it is the most precious! Whatever your image is in this respect, this is where you have to begin. If you are convinced of injustice so that you cannot see, even factually, that this conviction is wrong, the remedy is in finding in your own life how you have caused happenings that seem entirely unjust. The better you understand the magnetic force of images and the powerful strength of all psychological and unconscious currents, the better will you understand and experience the truth of these teachings, and the more deeply will you be convinced that there is no injustice. Find the cause and effect of your own inner and outer deeds.

So often man concentrates unduly on the apparent injustice that has come to him. He thinks and thinks again of how wrong others are. This should and can be recognized. But try to find how you have helped to bring this about. If you make half the effort you usually make finding others' faults to find your own, you will see the connection with your own law of cause and effect and this alone will set you free, will show you that there is no injustice. This alone will show you that it is not God, nor the fates, nor any unjust world order wherein you have to suffer the consequences of other people's shortcomings, but your ignorance, your fear, your pride, your egotism that directly or indirectly caused that which seemed, so far, to come your way without your attracting it. Find that hidden link and you will come to see truth. You will realize that you are not ever a prey to circumstances and other people's imperfections but really the master of your fate. You will deeply understand, not only in theory but in practice, that everything happening to you is a direct or indirect result of your attitudes, deeds, thoughts and emotions. Emotions are the most powerful of all, and this is constantly overlooked, even by my friends who have learned and at times experienced this truth. Your own unconscious affects the unconscious of the other person. This truth is perhaps most relevant to the discovery of how you call forth all happenings in your life, good or bad, favorable or unfavorable.

Once you experience this, you can dissolve your God-image, whether you fear God because you believe in injustice and are afraid of being the prey of circumstances over which you have no control; or whether you reject self-responsibility and expect an indulgent, pampering god to lead life for you, make decisions for you, take self-inflicted hardships from you. The realization of how you cause the effects of your life will dissolve either God-image. This is one of the main breaking-points.

One of the handicaps is your guilt feeling, or rather your wrong attitude toward guilt. In order to understand that, it might be advisable to reread my lecture on the subject of justified and unjustified guilt feelings and the proper attitude toward shortcomings. If your faults depress you so deeply that you are afraid to face them, then this wrong attitude has to be worked on first because it hinders you in coming out of your own vicious circle. The guiltier you feel about possible wrongs you may have to face, the more you escape reality and thereby inflict harm on your soul. The proper and constructive attitude toward your own shortcomings is the key to the dissolution of this and all other vicious circles you may be caught in. Understand that none of your faults exist out of malice or because you wish something evil on other people. All faults, every kind of selfishness, is nothing but a misunderstanding and a wrong conclusion. Your fear often makes you so paralyzed that your proper faculties cannot function. Thus you do not see or react properly and this brings effects into your life which you no longer connect with the origin of your fear and the then resulting errors in judgment, action and reaction on your part. But so long as you shy away from facing your erroneous reactions because of a faulty attitude toward your shortcomings, you cannot find the breaking-point.

This breaking-point alone will bring you the recognition that you are not a victim, that you have the power over your life, that you are free, and that these laws of God are infinitely good, wise, loving and safe! They do not make a puppet out of you but make you wholly free and independent.

In order to help you find the proper concept of God, I will try to speak about Him. But remember that all words can at best be only a small point to start with in cultivating your own inner recognition. Words are always insufficient; how much more insufficient they are in the attempt to describe God Who is unexplainable, Who is all things, Who cannot be limited with words. How can your perception and capacity to understand suffice to sense the greatness of the Creator? Every smallest inner deviation and obstruction is a hindrance to understanding. We have to be concerned with the elimination of these hindrances, step by step, stone by stone, for only then will you glimpse the light and sense the infinite bliss.

One hindrance is that despite the teachings you have received from various sources, you still unconsciously think about God as a person who acts, chooses, decides, disposes arbitrarily and at will. On top of this you superimpose the idea that all this must be just. But even though you include justice, this idea is false. For God is. His laws are made once and for all and work automatically, so to speak. Emotionally you are somehow bound to this wrong concept, and it stands in your way. As long as it is present, the real and true concept cannot fill your being.

God is, among so many other things, life and life force. Think of this life force as you think of an electric current, endowed with supreme intelligence. This "electric current" is there, in you, around you, outside of yourself. It is up to you how you use it. You can use electricity for constructive purposes, even for healing, or you can use it to kill. That does not make the electric current good or bad. You make it good or bad.

This power current is an important aspect of God and is the one which touches you most. This concept may raise the question whether God would thus be entirely impersonal and therefore to be feared even more. It may seem to contradict the idea of His infinite love. Neither is true.

God, being all, is personal if He chooses to be, but His personal aspect has no bearing on the question we are now discussing and on one of the most important aspects of your personal life.

His love is not only personal in God-manifest, but also in His laws, in the being of the laws. The apparent impersonal love in the laws that are— understand what is implied in the words "that are"—shows in the fact that they are made in such a way that they lead you ultimately into light and bliss, no matter how much you deviate from them. The more you deviate from them, the more do you approach them by the misery that the deviation inflicts. This misery will cause you to turn around at one point or another. Some sooner, some later, but all must finally come to the point where they realize that they themselves determine their misery or bliss. This is the love of the law. Deviation from the law is the very medicine to cure deviation and therefore it brings you closer to the goal.

The love of the law—and therefore of God—is also contained in the fact that God lets you deviate if you wish; that you are made in His likeness, meaning that you are completely free to choose as you wish. You are not forced to live in bliss and light though you can if you wish. All this means the love of God. It is not easy to understand, but those of you who have difficulty in understanding will one day see the truth of these words.

When you have difficulty in understanding the justice of the universe and self-responsibility in your life, do not think of God as "He"—although, of course, God can manifest as a person too, since He can do anything and is Everything. Rather think of God as the Great Creative Power at your disposal. It is not God who is unjust, as your subconscious may believe, but it is your wrong use of the powerful current at your disposal. If you go on from this premise and meditate on it and from there on to seek where you have ignorantly abused the power current in you, God will answer you. This I can promise you. If you sincerely search for this answer and if you have the courage to face it without the wrong kind of guilt feelings—and you should all be big enough for that by now—you will come to understand the cause and effect in your life that led you to believe (be it until now unconsciously, but because of that all the more powerfully) that God's world is a world of cruelty and injustice; a world in which you have no chance, a world in which you have to be afraid and hopeless; a universe where God's grace comes to a few chosen ones, but you are excluded. Only this can free you of this fallacy that distorts your soul and your life.

I know, you do not think all that. But many of you feel it deeply hidden in your subconscious. Try to find that part in you where you do feel that way, regardless of your simultaneously sincere love for God. Find out whether you do not fear God more than you love Him. If you do, you can be sure this image of God exists in you, and you are living by distortion and illusion since all images are just that. Enumerate the injustices in your own life—do not go into the lives of others or general conditions, for there you cannot find the answer—and then try to find where you have abused the power current and connect these instances with the injustices. If you cannot do so right away, I will help you and further work will show it to you quite clearly, provided you truly desire to find the answers. You have no idea what this discovery will mean to you. The greater the resistance to it first, the greater the victory! You have no idea how free it will make you, how safe and secure; you will fully understand the marvel of the creation of these laws that let you, with the power current of life, do as you please regarding your own life. This will give you confidence and the deep, absolute knowledge that you have nothing to fear.

There is a type of personality so negative in this respect that he is deeply convinced of the futility of life—perhaps only in the subconscious— and that the available life force can work only in a negative way. This may sound like a paradox, my friends, but it is not. Life force is energy, and the energy at your disposal in a personality problem of this type is used only negatively. That means, for instance, that the person becomes alive mostly in negative situations; in situations of fight, unrest, quarrel, and disharmony of any kind. Then something vibrates inwardly. Yet, when everything goes smoothly, although a part of the personality may enjoy it (usually the more conscious side), another part feels deflated and lifeless. This comes from the fact that the distortion in the God-image has progressed to a considerable degree. Most people have it to a smaller degree, at least occasionally. Examine your reactions with regard to feeling more alive in a negative situation and more dead in a quiet one. You will find therein the connection with your God-image.

Are there any questions regarding this subject?

QUESTION: Could you give us some examples of abuse of the life force?

ANSWER: Abuse of the power currents of your life force is all actions, deeds, thoughts, attitudes and all emotions deviating from divine truth that are self-directed, that are motivated by separateness.

QUESTION: What does that mean?

ANSWER: I have discussed separateness frequently in the past. Separateness of the soul, briefly, is created when a person withdraws inwardly, puts an invisible wall around his soul in the mistaken idea that it is safe to do so. This is, for instance, a strategy of people who are afraid of life and love, afraid of reality, afraid of self-responsibility. All that leads to separateness. All this actually means is that the person considers himself to be different than others. The bridge to brotherhood is eliminated. This may happen in all sorts of reactions where it is not always obvious. Each human fault contributes to separateness and is of itself a wrong conclusion and therefore a falsity, an illusion. If you analyze each fault, you will find that it exists because it is thought to be protective and advantageous. In truth it is not, for nothing can be to your advantage that is to the disadvantage of another person. Such is separateness; separateness is an illusion of the world of manifestation.

QUESTION: The question was asked by someone who is absent, about the connection of the interplay on the human plane of action and reaction in connection with God's will, the will of the higher self, free will and self-will.

ANSWER: The will of the higher self is God's will. There is no difference. Free will may be God's will or it may be self-will. It can be either since it is free. Even the self-will may correspond to God's will, only the motive varies. In other words, the goal may be right, only God's will is relaxed, is patient, is not concerned with one's ego. God's will is flexible, while self-will may want to attain the same results but is rigid, impatient, self-concerned.

Interaction, action and reaction, from one person to the other, that goes into a much more complicated problem. I suspect that the question was asked with the perhaps not entirely conscious idea, "Am I dependent on another person's error made with his free will?" "If my neighbor chooses with his free will to commit a wrong deed, and I am affected by it, how do I come by it? Do I deserve it? Am I not then a victim of the arbitrary choice of free will or self-will of my fellow creatures?"

This is a very important human problem that colors one's attitude to life; man has a deeply hidden fear of his dependence on other people's choice in action and motive. I realize it is very difficult for you to grasp and understand that you are never, never dependent on another person, even if it seems that way. That is the illusion of the world of manifestation. The teachings and the path I show you must prove to you forever more that it is you yourself who inflict difficulties, conflicts and hurts on yourself, no matter how much the other person may be at fault. If you are free of images, illusions, wrong conclusions and wrong concepts, the wrong deeds of others can never affect you. You will then learn to adjust to the world and the happy or unhappy incidents in your life; favorable or unfavorable happenings will have exactly the same effect on you. Of course you are not that far yet, but by slow degrees you approach it. And some of my friends, be it only for a short instant, have already experienced this truth, this great truth, although afterward it may evaporate again. Once experienced, you will find it easier to recapture this knowledge and build on it.

And so, my dearest friends, may the words I gave you tonight bring light into your soul, into your life. Let them fill your heart. Let them be an instrument to liberate you from illusions, my dearest friends. I bless each one of you, individually and as a whole. God's world is a wonderful world and there is only reason to rejoice on whatever plane you live, whatever illusions or hardships you temporarily endure. Let them be a medicine for you and grow strong and happy with whatever comes your way. Be blessed. Be in peace. Be in God!

Unity and Duality

GREETINGS, my dearest friends. May this evening be a blessing and an enrichment for every one of you here and for all those who read these words. May you open your minds and your hearts so that you understand them deep within yourself; if you do not understand immediately, these words may take root in your psyche and come to fruition later. Full understanding of this lecture may reach you only as you work your way through the deep layers of your unconscious where what I say here finds application.

There are two basic ways for man to live, to approach life and himself. Or, to put it differently, there are two fundamental possibilities regarding consciousness in the human being: dualistic and unified consciousness. The majority of human beings live predominantly on the dualistic plane of consciousness. This means that man sees, perceives, and experiences everything in opposites—either/or, good or bad, right or wrong, life or death. In other words, in practically everything man encounters, in every human problem and predicament, his approach is determined by this dualistic way of perceiving life.

The unified principle combines the opposites of the dualistic plane. When dualistic consciousness is transcended, the pain of living in dualism no longer exists. Few human beings transcend the dualistic plane or experience even occasionally a taste of the wide, limitless outlook, the wisdom and freedom of the unified plane.

In the unified plane of consciousness there are no opposites. There is no good vs. bad, no right vs. wrong, no life vs. death. There is only good, only right, only life. Yet this is not the kind of good or the kind of right or the kind of life that comprises but one of the opposites of the dualistic plane: it transcends both and is of a completely different nature. That good or that right or that life which exists on the unified plane of consciousness combines both aspects of the dualistic way of life. In the unified state of mind, no conflict exists because the dualism is combined and the opposites no longer conflict with one another.

To live in a unified state, in absolute reality, is the bliss, the unlimited freedom, the fulfillment and the unlimited realization of potentials that religion calls heaven. Heaven is usually thought to be a place in time and space, though of course, this is not so. It is a state of consciousness which can be realized at any time in whatever shape an individual entity exists. By this I mean a human being in the flesh as well as one who does not live in a material body. The unified state of consciousness is a question of understanding or, as I often refer to it, of "knowingness."

On the dualistic plane life must be a continuous problem. Man's struggle is in coping with the arbitrary and illusory division of the unified principle; things become opposites and that imposes conflicts. It creates tension and struggle within man and therefore with the outer world.

Let us understand this particular struggle a little better, and therefore the human predicament. Regardless of how asleep, of how unconscious, of how ignorant man may be of it, there nevertheless is such a thing as a unified state of mind, or a real self which is and lives in him and expresses and manifests the unified principle. Even those who have never heard of such a thing, who are utterly ignorant of the terms or of their meaning, have a deep longing and a deep, mostly unconscious sense of a different state of mind, a hope of experiencing life in a different way than the one they know. They yearn for the state of freedom, the blissfulness, and the mastery of life that the unified state of consciousness affords.

This longing is, however, misinterpreted by the personality. It is misinterpreted partly because it is an unconscious yearning for what may usually be called "happiness" or "fulfillment." What is really meant by these words is a state of unification of the opposites that exist on the dualistic plane so that there is no longer any struggle or effort, no fight, no tension, no conflict, no anxiety or fear. Consequently, the world is alive and the self is master. Not master in a tight, tense, hostile way, but master in a way such that life can be exactly what the individual determines it to be. This freedom and this mastery and this bliss and this liberation from tension and agitation in the human soul are consciously and unconsciously longed for and striven for.

Man often misinterprets this longing, partly because the knowledge of its nature is lacking; it is only a vague feeling deep within the soul. Even when the theoretical knowledge of such a state exists, it is still mostly misinterpreted for yet another reason: when freedom and mastery, unification and its resulting bliss, and the manifestation of the unified state of consciousness are striven for and attempted on the dualistic plane, tremendous conflict must ensue. This is what mostly happens: man strives for the fulfillment of his deep longing to transcend and find, deep within himself, a new state of consciousness in which all is one. When he seeks this on a plane where all is divided, not only can he never find what he seeks, but he must despair and split himself further apart in conflict because, as I have often said, illusion creates duality. This is overwhelmingly the case with people who are ignorant of these possibilities. It is also true of people who are more spiritually enlightened but are nevertheless ignorant of the distinct difference between these two planes and who do not see how in themselves and in their practical daily existence they can learn to transcend the dualistic plane.

When the vague longing for, or the precise theoretical knowledge of, the unified plane of consciousness is misread; when man knows and senses that there is only good, freedom, right, beauty, love, truth, life, without a threatening opposite, but then tries to apply this on the dualistic plane, he will immediately be plunged into the very conflict of opposites he seeks to avoid. He must then fight for one of the dualistic aspects and against the other, and such a fight makes transcendence impossible.

Let me demonstrate this in terms of a familiar everyday human problem so that you can apply and understand these words in more than their abstract meaning. Man finds himself constantly plunged into conflict with those in his surroundings. Let us assume a person is in a quarrel with a friend. He is convinced from where he sits that he is right. Therefore, immediately, the friend becomes wrong. With man's dualistic understanding it can only be an either/or. The outcome seems to matter more than the particular issue; when the intensity of emotions is measured, it often is out of proportion to the issue at stake. It is commensurate with a life or death matter. Although man may think this irrational on a conscious level, unconsciously he feels that being wrong truly means being dead, for being wrong means to be denied by the other.

On the dualistic plane, man's sense of identity is associated with the other person, not with his real self. As long as man experiences himself only as the outer ego-self, he must depend on others, as I shall explain in greater detail a little later. When man has realized the center of his being, which is unification, only then does his life no longer depend on others. Hence, a slight quarrel becomes truly a matter of life or death. This explains the intensity of emotions and the intensity of the need to prove that he is right and the other is wrong.

On the dualistic plane each issue ends with either life or death. Life becomes so important in order to avoid death, while death is so feared that one runs into it head on. Such a constant struggle with life—a result of the struggle against death—renders people sufficiently unhappy to believe that they do not fear death. In any issue you happen to be involved in, as long as you feel that you must win, that one view is so while the other is not so, you are deeply involved in the world of duality and therefore in a world of illusion and therefore in constant strain and suffering, conflict and confusion. The more you fight in this way, the greater the confusion becomes.

Man is geared and trained in his upbringing, in everything he learns, absorbs, and perceives in his surroundings, to fight for one and against the other of any number of opposites. This not only applies to material issues and physical manifestations, but even more to the subtle plane of concepts and understanding.

As I have so often demonstrated, every truth can be divided into two opposites, one proclaimed as the "right idea," the opposite aspect declared as the "wrong idea," while, in reality, they complement one another. On the unified plane of truth and fulfillment, neither aspect is thinkable without the other; complements are "enemies" only on the dualistic plane of consciousness.

Every conflict snowballs into intricate sub-conflicts, subdivisions of the primary dualistic split. Since all this is a product of illusion, the further the conflict goes, the smaller the possibility that it can be resolved and the more hopelessly enmeshed man becomes. Let us now return to our example and demonstrate how this is so. The more the man strives to prove his friend wrong, the more friction is created. He believes that by proving himself right and the friend wrong, the friend will finally accept and love him again and all will be well. When this does not occur, he misinterprets it and tries harder; he thinks he has not sufficiently proven that he is right and the other is wrong. The rift widens and his anxiety increases. The more weapons he uses in his effort to win the fight, the deeper into difficulty he gets, until he actually damages himself and the other and acts against his own best interest. He is now faced with a further conflict which has arisen out of the first error and dualistic split. In order to avoid a total rift, with all its real and imagined dangers—for real damage has begun to be wrought—he is now faced with the alternatives of having to give in to appease and avoid damage to himself, or to continue fighting. Since he is still convinced that there is a right and a wrong, appeasement robs him of self-respect. Whether he uses this "solution" or not, he will be torn between the two alternatives: fighting or submitting. Both create tension, anxiety, and inner and outer disadvantages.

Thus a new duality develops out of the first. The original duality lies in the question of who is right and who is wrong with the insistence that "only I must be right, otherwise all is bad." The second lies in the necessity of giving in and assuming a wrong that one cannot admit, or continuing to fight. Admitting a wrong means death, in a sense. So one is faced with either admitting a wrong, which means death in the deep psyche, in order to avoid dreaded consequences and the possibility of a real risk—also death, in the deepest sense—or insisting that he is totally right. Any way he turns he finds death, disaster, loss, annihilation. The harder he fights for and against, the less there is to fight for and the more against him all alternatives become. The illusion that one side is good and the other bad inevitably leads to the next step on this road of illusion, which is that all is bad. All dualistic struggle leads into further traps which are all products of illusion.

When the road to the unified principle is chosen, what first appeared as one good opposed to one bad soon ceases to seem so and one inevitably encounters good and bad on both ends. When this "road" is pursued still further, there is no longer any bad, but only good. The road leads deep inside, into the real self, into truth that surpasses the fearful little ego's interests. When this truth is sought deep inside of the self, one approaches the unified state of consciousness.

Our example is a banal one and can be translated into many, many everyday issues. It exists in a small squabble between mates. It exists in a conflict between two countries at war. It exists in all mankind's difficulties, individual and collective. As long as a person finds himself in this dualistic, illusory conflict, there must be hopelessness, for there is no way out on the dualistic plane of thinking. As long as man's very existence is identified with the ego-self and therefore with the dualistic approach to life, he cannot help but despair, no matter how much this despair is covered up or momentarily alleviated by occasionally "winning" with the desirable alternative of the two opposites. The helplessness and hopelessness, the wasted energy of the dualistic struggle rob man of his birthright. This birthright he can only find on the plane of unification.

Since all rules and precepts, everything man learns and absorbs in his education and environment is geared to dualistic standards, it is not surprising that he is totally attached and adapted to this state of consciousness. Even when he learns and hears about this other possibility, he is frightened of it. He cannot believe in it and clings to what he knows. Here a vicious circle exists in that the dualistic rules and precepts which condition man to this way of life are in themselves a result of man's fear of giving up the egotistical state, which alone seems to guarantee him life. It appears to him that giving up this ego-state means annihilation of his individuality which, of course, is utterly erroneous. So, man has these rules because of his erroneous fears, and he clings to the false fears because of his indoctrination.

Before we discuss in greater detail why man clings to the painful dualistic state in spite of the immediate and direct possibility of unified consciousness, I would like to say more about the latter and discuss how to realize it within yourself. What we call the real self, or the divine substance in man, or the divine principle, or the infinite intelligence, or any number of other names mankind has chosen for the deep inner live center exists in every human being. It contains all wisdom and truth that man can possibly envisage. The truth is so far-reaching and so directly accessible that no further conflict exists where and when this truth is allowed to take effect. The ifs and buts of the dualistic state of life cease to exist.

The knowing of this inborn intelligence is of such a nature that it surpasses the ego-intelligence. It is completely objective as it disregards small, vain self-interest; this is one of the reasons it is feared and man avoids contact with it. The truth that flows out of it equalizes the self with others in a way that not only is not the annihilation that the ego fears, but that opens up a storehouse of vibrant life force and energy. Man usually draws on this energy only to a minor degree and he misuses it in directing his attention and his hopes to the dualistic plane—the plane of the ego with its tightly held opinions, conclusions, false ideas, vanity, with its pride, self-will and fear. When this live center activates man, he begins his limitless unfolding; these accomplishments become possible precisely because the little ego no longer needs them for its enhancement in order to live on the dualistic plane.

The unified real self can always be contacted, in every issue of man's life. Let us again return to our example in order to see exactly how this could be done in such a case. The act which appears to be the most difficult for a man to perform but which, in reality, is the easiest and most unstrained act possible, is to ask, "What is the truth of the matter?" The moment an individual is more bent on the truth than on proving that he is right, he contacts the divine principle of transcendent, unified truth. If the desire to be in truth is genuine, inspiration must come forth. No matter how much circumstances seem to point in one direction, man must be willing to relinquish and question that what he sees is all there is to the issue. This generous act of integrity opens the way to the real self. This act will be easier to perform when man contemplates that it is not necessarily a question of either/or, but that there may be aspects of right in the other and of wrong in himself that, so far, he has not seen because his attention was not directed to this eventuality. With this approach to a problem, man immediately opens the way to enter into the unified plane of existence and to be moved by the real self.

This immediately releases an energy which is distinctly felt when this act is committed in a deep and sincere way. It also brings release of tension. What he then finds out is always totally different from both what he hoped for and feared on the dualistic plane. He finds that he is not as right and innocent as he thought, nor as wrong as he feared, nor is the opponent. He soon discovers aspects in the matter that he never saw before, although they were not necessarily concealed. He understands exactly how the quarrel came into existence in the first place, what led to it, its history before its actual manifestation. With this he gains insight into the nature of the relationship, he learns about himself and the other and he increases his understanding of the laws of communication. The more vision he thus gains, the freer, stronger, and more secure he feels. Such vision not only eliminates the particular conflict, showing the right way and approach to straighten it out, but also reveals important aspects of the person's general difficulties, the elimination of which becomes easier through understanding this experience.

The vibrant peace that comes through this extended understanding is of lasting value. It affects man's efforts toward self-realization and has beneficial results in his daily life as well. This is a typical example of unified, intuitive understanding and knowing the truth. After the initial apparent need for courage and the momentary resistance to seeing a wider truth than that of the ego, living with the truth is much easier than the struggle that ensues on the either/or plane of life.

Before you can bring yourself to this way of thinking and being, the tension will mount. As long as you are still on the dualistic plane, you struggle against this way of thinking because you believe falsely that the moment you admit and see wrong in yourself and right in the other, you submit and enslave yourself. You become nothing, worthless, pitiful, and from there, in your fantasy life, it is only a step to annihilation. Hence, you feel it as the greatest of dangers to leave the dualistic plane. The more the conflicts tear you in several directions at once, the more the tension mounts. The moment you are willing to be in truth, the moment you are eager and prepared, not merely to see your way, your little truth, or to give in to the other's little truth in fear of the consequences if you do not; when you wish to be in possession of the larger, more encompassing truth which transcends both of your little truths, in that moment a specific tension will be released in your psyche. The way toward the manifestation of the real self will be prepared.

Let me repeat here what I have often mentioned before. The two most significant obstructions to the real self are ignorance of its existence and of the possibility of connecting with it, and a tight, cramped psychic state with tight cramped soul movements. These two factors make contact impossible with the real self, and therefore with a unified state of existence. As long as you are on the dualistic plane, you must constantly be in a soul cramp. You may remember how often I discussed the importance of observing your soul movements. When you fight against one dual aspect and press for the other, observe the soul movements coming forth. Superficially, you may lean on the apparent justification of what you press for. You may say, "Is it not perfectly justified and right that I am against this wrong in the world?" On the dualistic plane this may indeed be so. But in this limited outlook you ignore the fact that this wrong exists only because of the dualistic approach to the problem and the prevalent ignorance that there is another approach. The tension of opposition blurs the view that other aspects exist which unify that which you deem right and that which you deem wrong.

Wholly wanting the truth requires the willingness to relinquish what one holds on to, whether this be a belief, a conviction, a fear, a cherished way of being. When I say relinquish, I merely mean questioning it and being willing to see that there is something else beyond it. This brings us back to what I said I would discuss, namely, why man is so terrified to relinquish the ego-state and hence the painful dualistic way of life. Why does he so much fear and resist entrusting and committing himself to the deep inner center which is a reality, which combines and unifies all good, and which is instantly accessible? It is, however, beyond the personal, little considerations of the ego.

As I have said, the dualistic plane is the plane of the ego, whereas the unified plane is the world of the divine center, of the larger self. The ego's whole existence is on the plane where it is at home. To give up operating on this plane means to give up the claims of the little ego. This does not mean its annihilation, but to the ego it seems to mean this. Actually, the ego is a particle, an isolated aspect of the vaster intelligence, of the real, inner self. It is not different from it, but there is less of the real self in it. Since it is separated, disconnected, and limited, it is less reliable and secure than that from which it stems. But this does not mean that it needs to be annihilated. In actual fact, it will integrate with the real self so that there is one being which is fuller, better equipped, wiser, with more and better of all assets imaginable.

The separated ego thinks this means annihilation, ceasing to exist. In its ignorant, limited way, it feels its existence only as a separated being, hence it pursues further separateness. I know that I have said all this many times before, but in the context of this lecture it is once again important to think about and apply this. Since consciousness is ignorant of the existence of the real self—even if it is accepted as a theory, its living reality must be doubted as long as personal misconceptions are not eliminated—it fears the soul movement of letting go and relaxing the tight hold, which leads to the realization of the real self. This is the constant dilemma of the ego until it ceases fighting against the recognition of a wider truth in every smallest personal issue.

As you have heard me say many times, the real self cannot manifest as long as personal inner difficulties and problems are not straightened out. But the process of doing this and the first inklings of self-realization often overlap; the one furthers the other. This specific way of looking at your basic human struggle may help you considerably.

As long as man is totally identified with his separated ego, he must, as I said, cultivate more separation, hence self-idealization must be the consequence. Self-glorification and idealization is, from this point of view, your apparent salvation and the guarantee necessary to assuage your existential fears. The ego thinks, "If everyone around me thinks that I am special, then I will receive the necessary approval, love, admiration, agreement that I need in order to live." This applies whether you are especially good, or smart, or beautiful, or talented, or happy, unhappy, or even bad, or whatever specialty you have chosen for your self-glorification. This means that somewhere deep down, you believe that you can exist only through being noticed, affirmed, and confirmed by others. You feel that if you go unnoticed, if no one knows of your existence, you cease to live. This may sound exaggerated but it is not. It explains why some people's idealized self-image is destructive and negative. They feel more confident about making themselves noticed through negative qualities than through positive specialness.

Your salvation seems to lie in others who acknowledge your existence only if you are different, special. At the same time, the misinterpreted message from the real self is a desire to master life, so you master it on the wrong plane and believe that you must vanquish all resistance that is put in your way. Each personal pseudo-solution is a way in which you hope to eliminate the obstructions put in your way. The pseudo-solution you choose depends on individual character traits, on circumstances and early influences. Whatever they are—and you know that there are three basic ones: the aggressive, the submissive and the withdrawal solutions—they are destined to assure your triumph over others and establish your "freedom" and "fulfillment." Your existence seems to be guaranteed when you are totally loved, accepted, and served by others and this you hope to attain by triumphing over them.

You can see that you are governed by a succession of wrong conclusions. Of course, you can ascertain that all these reactions and beliefs exist in you only when you have learned to admit them, when you question the meaning of each particular reaction and look behind the facade and beyond what you pretend it means. Once this step is taken, it is easy to verify that all these misconceptions govern you and rob you of the beauty of reality. You will further come to see—not as a theory, but as a reality experienced—that your life does not depend on others' affirmation of your existence; that you do not need to be special and separated from others; that this very claim traps you in loneliness and confusion; that others will give you love and acceptance only when you do not wish to be better than they are, or special or different from them. This love will come when your very life no longer depends on it.

When you have truly attained knowledge, when you are truly accomplished in whatever field it may be, it cannot have the effect on others that it has when accomplishment serves to set you apart. In the one case your accomplishment will be a bridge to others, because it is not a weapon against them. In the other instance it will create antagonism because you wish to be accomplished in order to be better than others—which always means that others must be less. When you need to be better than others through your accomplishments, what you give to the world must turn against you because you offer it in a spirit of war. When you offer your accomplishments to enrich life and others, you and your life will be enhanced by it because what you offer is given in a spirit of peace. In the latter case, you become a part of life. In taking from life—the live center within yourself—and giving back to life as an integral part of it, you act according to the unified principle.

Whenever the struggle exists, "In order to live I must be better than others, I must be separate," disappointment is inevitable. It cannot bring the desired result because it is based on illusion. The dualistic concept is "me versus the other." It is this illusory belief which makes the transition from the dualistic to the unified plane of consciousness so difficult, for giving up this fight-against-the-other appears to imply the annihilation of self. The more one fights against the other, the less he will accept the need to affirm his real self and the more will this probability be experienced as a danger equal to completely giving up the fight. Every way man turns seems to be blocked. He makes himself utterly dependent on others due to the misconception that otherwise he is lost, while at the same time trying to overrun and triumph over them. He must resent the dependency and feel guilty about the triumph. While both create intense frustrations and anxiety, neither yields any salvation whatever.

Notice the initial disinclination to question your assumptions concerning any problematic issue in your life. The outer quarrel or issue is so painful because the inner struggle is between life and death—or so you believe. The illusory nature of this struggle can be established only when you dare to question your reactions honestly and precisely. Even though some of you are quite accomplished in this pathwork, in self-facing up to a degree, you still manage to bury the issue when it becomes really painful and frightening. This is your stumbling block because shying away from what appears so painful and frightening makes it impossible to uncover the fallacy of your hidden belief.

What you hold on to secretly, born out of your dualistic outlook and the ensuing inner battle, cramps your inner movement and debilitates you. It paralyzes your free flowing energies and makes the transition to the unified plane impossible.

When you look at your problems from an objective and detached point of view, from the wider outlook of the real self, when you turn your best intent and will to the matter that disturbs you in a genuine wish for impartiality, you will first notice a shrinking back from such a desire and a more or less overt or subtle covering up of your desire for flight. Catch yourself in this act and courageously forge on, questioning yourself further and deeper. You will then come to see that, finally, the outer quarrel or difficulty is a symbolic representation of the inner quarrel in you in which you fight for life against death, for existence against annihilation. You will see what you believe is required from others in order for you to exist. When you have arrived at this level of your being, you will be able to question the precepts that served as the foundation for this. And this is the first step toward the transition from dualistic error into unified truth.

You will further notice that relinquishing ideas, ideals, and convictions also feels like annihilation, for being wrong means dying, being right means living. The moment you go through this opening-up movement and have the courage to want the truth, you can envisage the possibility of a wider and more complete truth than you can see at the moment in whatever the issue is. You will then come to a new peace and a new intuitive knowledge about the way things are. Something in your hardened psychic material will have loosened up and this further prepares the way for total self-realization. Each time you loosen up, your way will become a little easier and the climate in your psyche will be more favorable to the final total awakening into your inner center of all life, all truth, of the unified good of creation.

Every step in this direction is based on abandoning another misconception, and each misconception represents another burden. The giving up of what first seemed like security and protection from annihilation will now be disclosed as what it really is: burden, suffering, imprisonment. You will then comprehend the preposterous fact that you are actually opposed to leaving the dualistic life with all its hardship, its hopelessness. Perhaps you can now understand some of this and this will help you in your personal path. When you apply this to your everyday life, you will see that the abstract-sounding words I use here are not something far away, but are accessible to every one of you. You will see that these words are practical and concrete, if you are willing to see yourself in relationship to life in a wider truth than you are as yet willing to even contemplate.

On the dualistic plane you must have everything your way. You must triumph over life, over others, over circumstances. You must prove yourself to be stronger than all other factors in your life which may oppose you. Opposition means that you may lose, and losing, in the last analysis, means your non-existence. That is what you are frightened of and why you struggle so intensely. That is why you always feel as though something much larger is at stake than the actual issue. This is why you deny the intensity of your emotions, knowing that what takes place on the conscious level is not commensurate with your real reactions.

If at times you win, is it really enduring peace you gain? Not really, my friends. At the moment, you may be gratified and appeased and feel safe. But how long can you remain master of your life under dualistic principles? The next issue endangers you all over again, and deep inside you know this, only you know it in the false way in which you believe it to be your undoing. You must therefore constantly live in fear that you cannot always win.

In this dependency in which life must always be according to your needs, or rather your imagined needs, so that you can master it, you must become resentful of those who prohibit your gratification. You must be resentful of life which seemingly does not let you be. The message coming from the real self says, "Your birthright is perfect happiness, freedom and mastery over life." When you fight for this birthright under dualistic principles, you remove yourself further and further from the realization of your self, in which you could truly have mastery, freedom and total fulfillment. You seek all this with false means which are as varied as are individuals and their characters.

In all these years we have discussed many of these false means, the pseudo-solutions. If you restudy them in the light of this lecture, you will understand on a deeper level what this is all about. You will see how you personally try to win the fight, the false fight leading into more confusion and pain. The three basic pseudo-solutions are but means for conquering life on the dualistic plane so as to guarantee your existence. The submissive solution is just as opposed to truth and peace, not one iota less aggressive than the overt fight, because in submission the hostility always smolders underground. Whatever your ways to win, you are dependent on others and on circumstances often way beyond your actual control and therefore doomed to failure; this anxiety and futile struggle makes your psychic material brittle, hardened. The more this is so, the less are you able to contact the center of your inner being where all that you could possibly need is found: vital well-being and productivity and the peace of inner relaxation, which are integral by-products of the real self.

The only way you can truly enter into the unitive state of life in which you can truly be master is by no longer needing to triumph, to win, to be separate, to be special, to be right, to have it your way; by finding and discovering the good in all situations, whatever they are, whether you deem them good or bad, right or wrong. Needless to say, this does not mean resignation nor does it mean fearful giving in or weakness. It means going with the stream of life and coping with what is as yet beyond your immediate control, whether or not it is according to your liking. It means accepting where you are and what life is for you at this moment. It means being in harmony with your own inner rhythm. This will open the channel, so that finally total self-realization takes place. This means that all your expressions in life are motivated and lived through by the divine principle operating in you and expressing itself through your individuality, integrating your ego faculties with the universal self. This enhances your individuality, and does not diminish it. It enhances every one of your pleasures; it takes nothing away from you whatever.

May every one of you comprehend that the truth is in you; everything you need is in you. May you find that you actually do not have to fight and struggle as you constantly do. All you have to do is see and recognize the truth wherever you stand now. All you have to do at this time is recognize that there may be more than you now see, and call upon your inner center, allowing yourself to be open to its intuitive messages to you. May you find this possible exactly where you need it most, at this particular moment. Your gauge is always that which feels most uncomfortable and from which you are most tempted to look away. Be blessed, continue your wonderful path, that path which will bring you to the realization that you already have what you need and are where you need to be. You merely look away because you are geared in the opposite direction. Be in peace. Be in God.

The Idealized Self-Image

R E E T I N G S, God bless all of you, my dearest friends. Welcome are all my old and new friends gathered here.

Let us continue with the series of lectures to help you gain further insight into yourselves and therefore into life. The two preceding lectures dealt with the great duality, the struggle between life and death, the illusion that it is a question of either/or. The more one is involved in duality, the more one sees life in terms of extremes.

The question of happiness versus unhappiness is felt in two extremes, in terms of either/or, with happiness standing for life and unhappiness for death. While still struggling in this duality, it is impossible to experience and accept the realization that life brings both. This is often accepted and believed intellectually, but emotionally the feeling is, "If I am unhappy now, I must always be unhappy." Then the tragic, unnecessary, and destructive struggle against death or unhappiness begins.

The event of birth is a painful experience for the infant. Other painful experiences are bound to follow although pleasurable experiences occur as well. Since the knowledge of pain is always present, the fear of it creates a basic problem.

Now I would like to discuss the most important countermeasure to which man resorts in the false belief that it will circumvent unhappiness, pain, death, never realizing that this very countermeasure not only does not avoid, but rather brings on the very thing that is most dreaded. This universal pseudo-protection is the creation of the idealized self-image. I have discussed this topic quite frequently with friends in their private work, but could do so only to a limited extent. The reason I could not go into more detail or discuss it in the public lectures so far is obvious, my friends: it had to follow the last two lectures. If you do not fully understand your struggle with duality, you cannot fully understand the creation and the function of the idealized self-image.

The idealized self-image is supposed to be a means of avoiding unhappiness. Since unhappiness automatically robs a child of security, self-confidence is diminished in proportion to unhappiness, though this unhappiness cannot be measured objectively. What one person may be able to cope with quite well and does not experience as drastic unhappiness, another temperament and character feels to be dismal woe.

At any rate, unhappiness and lack of belief in oneself are interconnected. The creation of the idealized self-image serves to supply missing self-confidence and thereby gain pleasure supreme. At least this is the unconscious reasoning process and it is not altogether different from the truth.

In truth and reality, healthy and genuine self-confidence is peace of mind. It is security and healthy independence and allows one to achieve a maximum of happiness through developing his inherent talents, leading a constructive life, and entering into fruitful human relationships. But since the self-confidence established through the idealized self is artificial and not genuine, the result cannot possibly be what was expected. Actually the consequence is quite the contrary and frustrating because cause and effect are not obvious to the person. It may take him a great deal of life experience and inner will to find the truth about himself. Then and only then will he slowly discover the links between his unhappiness and his idealized self-image.

This is the work to be done by those who follow this path, and some of my friends have already made some preliminary discoveries in this direction, but there is much more to it. Even you who have gained some insight in this respect have barely scratched the surface. None of you has grasped the significance, the effects, the damages that follow in the wake of the idealized self-image. You have not even fully recognized its existence or in what particular way it manifests in your individual case. This requires a great deal of work for which all the preceding work was necessary. The dissolution of the idealized self is the only possible way to find your true self, to find serenity and self-respect and to live your life fully.

There is much to be said about this topic, but tonight I can only go into the barest fundamentals. As time goes on, I shall be more specific and go into further details, but the results and findings of your personal work in this respect are more important.

I have occasionally used the term "mask self" in the past. The mask self and the idealized self-image are really one and the same. The idealized self masks the real self. It pretends to be something you are not.

As a child, regardless of what your particular circumstances were, you were indoctrinated with admonitions on the importance of being good, holy, perfect. When you were not, you were often punished in one way or another. Perhaps the worst punishment was that your parents withdrew their affection from you; they were angry and you had the impression you were no longer loved. No wonder that "badness" associated itself with punishment and unhappiness, "goodness" with reward and happiness. Hence to be "good" and "perfect" became an absolute must; it became literally a question of life or death for you.

On the other hand, you knew perfectly well that you were not as good and as perfect as the world seemed to expect you to be. This truth had to be hidden; it became a guilty secret and you started to build a false self. This, you thought, was your protection and your means of attaining what you desperately wanted—life, happiness, security, self-confidence. The awareness of this false self began to vanish, but you were and are permanently permeated with the guilt of pretending to be something you are not. You strain harder and harder to become this false self, this idealized self. You were, and unconsciously still are, convinced that if you strain hard enough, one day you will be that self. But this artificial squeezing-into-something-you-are-not process can never attain genuine self-improvement, self-purification and growth, because you started building on an unreal self and left your real self out. In fact, you are desperately hiding it.

The idealized self-image may have many forms and facets. It does not always dictate standards of recognized perfection. Oh yes, much of the idealized self-image dictates highly moral standards, making it all the more difficult to question its validity. "But isn't it right to want to be always decent, loving, understanding; never to be angry; not wanting to have any faults; trying to attain perfection? Isn't this what we are supposed to do?" Such considerations will make it difficult for you to discover the compulsive attitude that denies present imperfection; the pride and lack of humility in which you cannot accept yourself as you are now; and above all, the pretense with its resulting shame, fear of exposure, secretiveness, tension, strain, guilt, anxiety.

It will take some progress in this work before you begin to experience the difference in feeling between the genuine desire to gradually work towards growth and the ungenuine pretense imposed upon you by the dictates of your idealized self. You will discover the deeply hidden fear in which you believe your world has come to an end if you do not live up to its standards. You will sense and know many other aspects of and differences between the genuine and the ungenuine self. And you will also discover what your particular idealized self demands.

But there are also facets of the idealized self, according to personality, life conditions, and early influences, which are not and cannot be considered good, ethical, or moral. Aggressive, hostile, proud, overambitious trends are glorified or idealized. It is true that behind all idealized self-images these negative tendencies exist. But they are hidden, and since they crassly contradict the morally high standards of the particular idealized self, they cause additional anxiety that the idealized self will be exposed as the fraud it is. The person who glorifies such negative tendencies, believing them to prove his strength and independence, his superiority and aloofness, will be deeply ashamed of the "goodness" another person's idealized self proclaims as a must, considering it to be weakness, vulnerability, and dependency in an unhealthy sense. It is entirely overlooked that nothing makes a person as vulnerable as pride. Nothing causes so much fear.

In most cases there is a combination of these two tendencies: overexacting moral standards impossible to live up to, and pride in being invulnerable, aloof, and superior. The coexistence of these mutually exclusive ways presents a particular hardship for the psyche. Needless to say, the conscious awareness of this contradiction is missing until this particular work in well in progress. There are many more facets, possibilities, individual pseudo-solutions combining all sorts of mutually exclusive behaviors. All this has to be found individually.

Let us now consider some of the general effects of the existence of the idealized self and some of the implications. Since the standards and dictates of the idealized self are impossible to realize and yet you never give up the attempt, you cultivate within yourself an inner tyranny of the worst order. Since you do not realize the impossibility of being as perfect as your idealized self demands, you never give up whipping yourself, castigating yourself, and feeling yourself a complete failure whenever it is proven that you cannot be so. A sense of abject worthlessness comes over you whenever you fall short of these fantastic demands and engulfs you in misery. This misery may at times be conscious but most of the time it is not. Even if it is, you do not realize the entire significance, the impossibility of your demands. When you try to hide your reactions to your own "failure," you take to special means to avoid seeing it. One of the most common devices is to project the blame for "failure" into the outer world, onto others, onto life. This we have discussed at length in the past, but you will now understand the deepest reasons for such projections.

The more you try to identify with your idealized self-image, the harder the disillusionment whenever life brings you into a position where this masquerade can no longer be maintained. Many a personal crisis is based on this dilemma and much less on outer difficulties. These difficulties then become an added menace, beyond their objective hardship. The existence of the difficulties is a proof to you that you are not your idealized self, and that robs you of the self-confidence you falsely tried to establish with the creation of the idealized self.

There are other personality types who know perfectly well that they cannot identify with their idealized self, but they do not know this in a healthy way. They despair. They believe they ought to be able to live up to it. Their whole life is permeated with a sense of failure, while the former type only experiences it on more conscious levels when outer and inner conditions culminate in showing up the phantom of the idealized self as what it really is—an illusion, a pretense, a dishonesty. It amounts to saying, "I know I am imperfect, but I make believe I am perfect." Not to recognize this dishonesty is comparatively easy when rationalized by conscientiousness, honorable standards and goals, and a desire to be good.

The genuine desire to better oneself leads one to accept the personality as it is now. If this basic premise is the main governing force of your motivation for perfection, any discovery of where you fall short of your ideals will not throw you into depression, anxiety, and guilt but rather strengthen you. You will not need to exaggerate the "badness" of the behavior in question, nor will you defend youself against it with the excuse that it is the fault of others, of life, of fate. You will gain an objective view of yourself in this respect and this view will liberate you. You will fully assume responsibility for the faulty attitude, being willing to take the consequences upon yourself. When you act out of your idealized self, you dread nothing more than that, for taking the responsibility for your shortcomings is tantamount to saying, "I am not my idealized self."

A sense of failure, frustration, and compulsion, as well as guilt and shame, are the most outstanding indications that your idealized self is at work. These are the only consciously felt emotions out of all those that lie hidden underneath.

The idealized self has been called into existence in order to attain self-confidence and therefore, finally, happiness, pleasure supreme. The stronger its presence, the more genuine self-confidence fades away. Since you cannot live up to its standards, you think even less of yourself than you originally did. It is therefore obvious that genuine self-confidence can only be established when you remove the superstructure which is this merciless tyrant, your idealized self.

Yes, you could have self-confidence if the idealized self were really you and if you could live up to these standards. Since this is impossible and since, deep down, you know perfectly well you are not anything like what you think you are supposed to be, with this "super self," you build up additional insecurity and further vicious circles come into existence. The original insecurity which was supposedly whisked away by the establishment of the idealized self, steadily increases. It snowballs and becomes worse and worse. The more insecure you feel, the more stringent the demands of the superstructure, the idealized self, the less are you able to live up to it and the more insecure you feel. It is very important to see this vicious circle. But this cannot be done until and unless you become fully aware of the devious, subtle, unconscious ways in which this idealized self-image exists in your particular case. Ask yourself in what particular areas it manifests. What cause and effect is connected with it?

A further and drastic result of this problem is the constantly increasing estrangement from the real self. The idealized self, as I said, is false; it is a rigid, artificially constructed imitation of a live human being. You may invest it with many aspects of your real being; nevertheless, it remains an artificial construction. The more you invest it with your energies, your personality, your thought processes, concepts, ideas and ideals, the more strength you take from that center of your being which alone is amenable to growth. This center of your being is the only part of you, the real you, that can live, grow, and be. It is the only part that can properly guide you. It alone functions with all your capacities. It is flexible and intuitive. Its feelings alone are true and valid even if, for the moment, they are not yet fully in truth and reality, in perfection and purity. But the feelings of the real self function in perfection relative to what you are now, not being able to be more in any given situation of your life. The more you take out of that live center in order to invest into the robot you have created, the more estranged you become from the real self and the more you weaken and impoverish it.

In the course of this work, you have sometimes come upon the puzzling and often frightening question: "Who am I really?" This is the result of the discrepancy and struggle between the real and the false self. Only upon solving this most vital and profound question will your live center respond and function to its full capacity; will your intuition begin to function to its full capacity; will you become spontaneous, free of all compulsions; will you trust in your feelings because they will have an opportunity to mature and grow. Feelings will become every bit as reliable to you as your reasoning power and your intellect.

All this is the final finding of self. Before this can be done, a great many hurdles have to be overcome. It seems to you that this is a life or death struggle. You still believe you need the idealized self in order to live and be happy. Once you understand that this is not so, you will be able to give up the pseudo-defense that makes it seem necessary to maintain and cultivate the idealized self. Once you understand that the idealized self was supposed to solve your problems, the particular problems in your life, above and beyond your need for happiness, pleasure, and security, you will come to see the wrong conclusion of this theory. Once you go a step further and recognize the damage it has wrought in your life, you will see it as the burden it is. No conviction, theory, or words you hear will make you give it up, but the recognition of what specifically it was supposed to solve and what damage it has done and is continuing to do will enable you to dissolve this image of all images.

Needless to say, you also have to recognize most particularly and in detail what your specific demands and standards are and further, you have to see their unreasonableness, their impossibility. When you have a feeling of acute anxiety and depression, consider the fact that your idealized self may feel questioned and threatened, either by your own limitation, by others, or by life. Recognize the self-contempt that underlies the anxiety or depression. When you are compulsively angry with others, consider the possibility that this is but an externalization of your anger with yourself for not living up to the standards of your false self. Do not let it get away with using the excuse of outer problems to account for acute depression or fear. Look into the question from this direction and new angle. Your private and personal work will help you in this direction. It is almost impossible to do it alone. Only after you have made substantial progress in this direction will you recognize that so many of these outer problems are directly or indirectly the result of the discrepancy between your capacities and the standards of your idealized self and how you deal with this conflict.

As you proceed in this particular phase of the work, you will come to understand the exact nature of your idealized self; your demands, your requirements of self and others in order to maintain the illusion. Once you fully see that what you regarded as commendable is really pride and pretense, you will have gained a most substantial insight that enables you to weaken the impact of the idealized self. Then and only then will you realize the tremendous self-punishment you inflict upon yourself. For whenever you fall short, as you are bound to, you feel so impatient, so irritated that it can snowball into fury and wrath at yourself. Oh, this fury and wrath is often projected on others because it is too unbearable to be aware of self-hate, unless one unrolls this whole process and sees it entire, in the light. Nevertheless, even if this hate is unloaded upon others, the effect on the self is still there and it can cause disease, accident, loss, and outer failure in many ways.

When you make the very first steps toward giving up the idealized self, you will feel a sense of liberation as never before. Then will you be truly born again; your real self will emerge. Then you will rest within your real self, centered within. Then you will truly grow, not only on the outer fringes that may have been free of the dictatorship of the idealized self, but in every part of your being. This will change many things. First will come changes in your reactions to life, to incidents, to yourself and others. This changed reaction will be astounding enough, but little by little, outer things also are bound to change. Your different attitude will cause new effects.

The overcoming of your idealized self means overcoming an important facet of the duality between life and death.

At present you are not even aware of the pressure of your idealized self, of the shame, humiliation, exposure you fear and sometimes feel, of the tension, strain, and compulsion. If you have an occasional glimpse of such emotions, you do not as yet connect them with the fantastic demands of your idealized self. Only after fully seeing these fantastic expectations and their often contradictory imperatives, will you relinquish them. The initial inner freedom gained in this way will allow you to deal with life and to stand in life. You will no longer have to hold on frantically to the idealized self.

The mere inner activity of holding on frantically to the idealized self generates a pervasive climate of holding on in general. This is sometimes lived out in external attitudes, but most often it is an inner quality or attitude. As you proceed in this new phase of your work, you will sense and feel this inner tightness and gradually you will recognize the basic damage of it. It makes the letting go of many an attitude impossible. It makes it unduly difficult to go through any change that would allow life to bring forth joy and a spirit of vigor. You keep yourself contained within yourself and thereby you go against life in one of its most fundamental aspects.

The words are insufficient; you have to sense rather what I mean. You will know exactly what I mean when you have weakened your idealized self by fully understanding its function, its causes and effects. Then you will gain the great freedom of giving yourself to life because you no longer have to hide something from yourself and others. You will be able to squander yourself into life, not in an unhealthy, unreasonable way, but healthily as nature squanders herself. Then and only then will you know the beauty of living.

You cannot approach this most important part of your inner work with a general concept. As usual, your most insignificant daily reactions considered from this viewpoint will yield the necessary results. So continue your self-search out of these new considerations and do not be impatient if it takes time and relaxed effort.

One more word: the difference between the real and the idealized self is often not a question of quantity, as regards the goodness or badness of an action, but rather one of quality. That is, the original motivation is different in these two selves. This will not be easy to see, but as you recognize the demands, the contradictions, the cause-and-effect sequences, the difference in motivation will gradually become clear to you.

Another important consideration is the time element. The idealized self wants to be perfect, according to its specific demands, right now. The real self knows this cannot be and does not suffer from this fact.

Of course you are not perfect in your real self. It is a complex of everything you are at the moment. Of course you have your basic egocentricity, but if you own up to it, you can cope with it. You can learn to understand it and therefore diminish it with each new insight. Then you will truly experience the truth that the more egocentric you are, the less self-confident you can be. The idealized self believes just the opposite. Its claims for perfection are motivated by purely egocentric reasons and this very egocentricity makes self-confidence impossible.

This great freedom of coming home, my friends, is finding your way back to the real you. The expression "coming home" has often been used in spiritual literature and teachings but it has been much misunderstood. It is often interpreted to mean the return into the spirit world after physical death. Much more is meant by coming home. You may die many deaths, one earth life after another, but if you have not found your real self, you cannot come home. You must be lost and remain lost until you find the way into the center of your being. On the other hand, you can find your way home right here and right now while you are still in the body. When you muster the courage to become your real self, even though it would seem to be much less than the idealized self, you will find out that it is much more. Then you will have the peace of being at home within yourself. Then you will find security. Then you will function as a whole human being. Then you will have eliminated the iron whip of a task master whom it is impossible to obey. Then you will know what peace and security really mean. You will cease, once and for all, to seek it with false means.

QUESTION: So the real self does not have two souls, no duality?

ANSWER: Of course not. The duality ceases to exist once you accept yourself as part good and part bad, as consisting partly of the higher and partly of the lower self. These two sides will be integrated and live in peace with one another once you accept yourself with both. And only then can the lower side gradually develop and grow out of its blindness. But as long as you do not reconcile yourself that you are both good and bad, as long as you battle against this "badness" and believe you can not tolerate it, duality exists. By accepting your lower self you can gradually overcome it and, as well, the duality between the higher and the lower self. By nonacceptance, you increase duality. This is the same question I discussed regarding life and death. By accepting death, the duality between life and death is gradually decreased until it disappears altogether. Struggling against death, as you struggle against your lower self, duality increases.

QUESTION: Could you tell us what Goethe meant with the saying, "Two souls dwell in my breast?"

ANSWER: It can be interpreted to mean the higher and lower self. And it can also be interpreted to mean the duality between the idealized and the real self. The lack of peace between the higher and the lower self brings the idealized self into existence. These two dualities are interdependent.

You see, the more the idealized self is put between the real self and life, the less can life grow, the more it shrinks and is prohibited from functioning.

May you all find truth and help and further enlightenment through the words I gave you tonight. However, you should understand and expect that a theoretical understanding, especially now, will avail you nothing. As long as these words remain theory, you will not be helped by them. When you begin or continue to work in this direction and allow yourself to feel and observe your emotional reactions as to this subject, then will you make substantial progress in your own liberation and self-finding in the truest sense of the word.

Now, my dearest ones, each one of you, receive our love, our strength, and our blessings. Be in peace; be in God!

Positivity and Negativity: One Energy Current

G R E E T I N G S, my dearest friends. May the blessings of creative intelligence existing all around and within you, strengthen and enlighten you so that these words will find an echo in you, and will serve as material to help you continue successfully on the path toward finding your real self.

Most of my friends have now reached a layer within themselves where they are face to face with their destructiveness. Many of you have come to this awareness. I am referring to more than the discovery of a mere emotion, the acknowledgment of a momentary hostility; I mean an overall, pervasive, essential, lingering destructiveness that has been dormant all along and merely covered up. It is quite a different experience to find this layer, to feel it and the condition you were in before your new awareness. You are now in a state in which you can observe yourself thinking, feeling and acting destructively, while before you were at best only theoretically aware of it and could merely surmise its presence by the unpleasant manifestations in your life. Now you are coping with the problem of how to get out of this condition.

You are puzzled, because you do not like being this way. You even know and comprehend quite profoundly that it is totally useless, senseless—that destructiveness does not serve one good purpose. Nevertheless, you find yourself in the situation of being unable to let go of this destructiveness. In order to be able to do so, it is necessary that you understand the nature of destructiveness much better than you do.

It is not easy to reach an awareness where you can see yourself think, feel, and act destructively; where you are further aware of the fact that this causes you misery, but are totally unable and unwilling to give up this way of being. I might say that it is a great measure of success, if this word can be used, to be aware. But to accomplish the second part of this particular phase of your evolution, the nature of destructiveness must be better understood. As usual, this necessitates some repetitions, without which the topic could not be addressed comprehensively.

Man's dualistic concept of life has a great deal to do with the lack of comprehension of his destructiveness. Mankind is geared to think of a destructive force as opposed to a constructive force. Even those of you who theoretically know quite well that there is no such division tend to think, "Here are my negative feelings. I wish I could have positive feelings instead." Or you think that after the negative emotions are dissipated, a new set of feelings will follow, as though this new set of feelings consisted of an entirely different energy or psychic material. When man speaks of the two forces, the two sets of feelings, it is a figure of speech, a way of expressing two different kinds of experiences. However, this figure of a speech is an expression of the dualistic misconception operative within man's consciousness.

Actually, there is only one power. This is very important to understand, my friends, particularly when you come to deal with your own destructiveness, your negativity. There is one life force which energizes every expression of life. The same life force can flow in a constructive, positive, affirming way, or it can turn into a destructive, negating current. In order to understand this process in a specific and personal way, I will discuss it from the point of view of man in relation to his life. I will not give a discourse on general spiritual principles here, but only touch upon them when it is necessary to the understanding of the whole topic.

First I will repeat that the life force as such, when untampered with, is totally constructive, totally good, totally positive and affirming. Therefore it produces total pleasure for any living, feeling, perceiving consciousness. The more fully this consciousness is developed, the fuller the pleasure it can experience from and through the pure life force, in whatever way this may find expression. The pure life force cannot be anything but beauty.

Every life organism tends to realize this potentiality in nature—a newborn baby, a plant, a cell. When this natural flow is interfered with, the energy current seeking expression is blocked and prohibited from flowing to its destiny; the natural flow is stopped by conditions. These may be either outer or inner conditions—or both. When the young child encounters conditions in the outer environment that prohibit the natural flow, the extent of the damage depends upon how free he is from inner blockages. If inner blockages exist and lie dormant because they have not been eliminated in previous existences, the outer negative conditions will create a severe blockage, freezing the floating energy current and petrifying it into a hardened psychic mass. When no previous blockages exist, the outer negative conditions will create only a temporary disturbance in the flow of the life force. Man's persistent problems in life are a result of such blocked energy. Unblocking can occur only when the relationship between the inner and the outer negative conditions responsible for the blockage are thoroughly understood. The child's immature ego faculties make adequately dealing with the negative condition impossible. An outer negative condition can therefore never be totally responsible for the condensation of energy, for the paralysis of the life stream. It can only be the final activating factor, bringing the dormant negative inner condition to the fore.

Where the outer negative conditions activate the dormant inner negative condition is the point at which the positive life force turns into a destructive non-life force. Feelings turn from love to fear and hostility, from trust to distrust and so on. Finally, as you know from a previous lecture, the negative power becomes so unbearable that the feelings connected with it are numbed altogether.

When a human being finds himself on such a path, it is very important for him to understand specifically that the negative emotion cannot be replaced by a different positive emotion. It must be reconverted to its original state. How do we go about this, my friends? Each individual must find the way to reconvert this energy flow into its original state. Each life manifestation you are going through that is unpleasant, unpleasurable, problematic, anxiety-producing, is the result of a repetition of the situation where for the first time in this life the positive pleasure force was blocked, hindered, prohibited and has therefore turned into unpleasure.

Now it cannot be stated accurately that in this unpleasure, pleasure is totally absent. I mentioned this before in a different context, but it is not sufficiently understood so I have come back to it and now discuss it from a new angle. When you find yourself stymied in your attempt to overcome negativity, it is extremely important to sense deep within yourself the pleasurable aspect involved in this negativity, regardless of how much pain exists in your surface consciousness. The difficulty of ridding yourself of destructiveness is, of course, also due to other reasons the existence of which you have already verified: the desire to punish or the forcing current. The idea is: "If I am sufficiently unhappy, that will show the world how wrong it is not to give me what I want." But these reasons do not constitute the deepest difficulty in dissolving negativity. It is necessary to sense, first intuitively, then to feel very specifically, that in your feelings about your negativity there is a dichotomy between pleasure and unpleasure.

This is understandable when you look at the process in terms of the explanation I have given. The pleasure principle cannot possibly be completely absent, even though it appears in its distorted form. Its basic ingredients must always remain, no matter how distorted the manifestation is and consequently how difficult it is to detect the original nature of the life current. This is precisely why negativity seems so difficult to transform. The pleasurable aspect of it always exists. When it is understood that only the form of expression must be changed, so that the identical life current reconverts itself, negativity can be left behind. When it is understood that the painful aspects of it can be abandoned while the pleasurable aspects grow stronger, negativity can transform itself. When it is understood that a new set of emotions will not come from out of nowhere, but that the same current will manifest differently, what seems hard will happen by itself.

When you thus meditate, it will become possible for you to be aware of the pleasure attached to your destructiveness. Instead of feeling guilty about this pleasure and consequently repressing it, you will be in a position to allow the current to unfold, express itself and reconvert itself. The attachment of or connection between pleasure and destructiveness has been instrumental in the widespread guilt feeling mankind has about all experiences of pleasure. This in turn is responsible for numbing all feelings, for how can pleasure be liberated from destructiveness if both are considered equally wrong? And yet, man cannot live without pleasure, even if he has to have it in secret, for life and pleasure are one and the same. When pleasure is linked to destructiveness, destructiveness cannot be given up; it feels as if life were given up. This brings about a situation such that on one level of his inner life, man holds on equally to pleasure and destructiveness, feeling guilty and afraid regarding both. On a more conscious level, he is numbed and feels little or nothing.

It is not sufficient to know this generally; this knowledge must be brought back to your specific circumstances. What is the other manifestation at this moment that causes you continuous anguish—not a momentary experience caused by a one-time condition that then dissolves when new conditions arise but rather the problems in your life that you cannot come to terms with? In order truly to resolve these conditions which we call images and which forever re-create similar conditions in new situations, the blocked and paralyzed energy must be made fluid again. And this can only happen when you begin, as the first step in this particular phase of your development, to ascertain the pleasurable aspect in your destructiveness. You must feel the pleasure attached to the unpleasure of the problem. This must be a distinct realization.

Since the pleasure current in the life force primarily manifests itself in man's life in what is referred to as "sexuality," destructive, blocked energy contains blocked sexual energy. It follows that outer problems must be symbolic or representative of how sexual energy was first blocked by outer conditions. The pain of this blockage has caused destructiveness which at the same time contains aspects of the pleasure principle. Therefore, every difficult situation in life represents a sexual fixation in the innermost psyche that man fears and runs away from. Because he does not face up to this and live it, the outer condition becomes unresolvable; the situation becomes more and more alienated from its inner cause where it is still enlivened by the pleasure aspect.

You on this path must therefore go back in, as it were, and permit yourself to feel the pleasure in the destructiveness. Then and only then will you truly comprehend the painful outer situation which, offhand, may have nothing to do with your emotional life or with any sexual problems. I have often mentioned that in man's most secret sexual fantasies lie the secrets of his conflicts, as well as the key to their resolution. When you find the parallel between the outer problem and the pleasure current in your sexuality, you will be able to make the frozen energy fluid again. This will enable you to dissolve the negativity, the destructiveness, and this of course is essential for the elimination of the outer problem.

The inability to feel the pleasure in the unpleasure is the result of your fighting against yourself and not liking yourself for this particular distortion. Consequently, there is denial, repression and further alienation from the nucleus, where these conditions can be experienced and gradually altered.

Every problem must have such a nucleus, where the original current has been blocked and is therefore distorted, and where the pleasure/unpleasure dichotomy produces an unconscious fixation of the pleasure experience on a negative situation. One then fights against this for any number of reasons, with the further consequence that outer problems begin to form, and then repeat and repeat. They cannot be overcome until this nucleus is experienced. This applies to all stubborn problems, whether or not they seem to have anything to do with sexuality.

Now my friends, this chain reaction I have just explained must be personally understood and worked through. You must stop running away from this distortion in yourself. You must allow yourself to see it, to let it unfold within you, live through it within yourself—and then you will see the dichotomy between pleasure and unpleasure. You will understand and experience why and how destructiveness, in whatever shape or form it is manifest in your life, seems so difficult to abandon. At the same time it will loosen up far more than before, when you tried to force it away without this understanding.

All this may sound very theoretical to the person who is still far from this point, but many of my friends are very near or are already at the point where these words can be used and put into action, into recognition. This will be a turning point in your inner and consequently your outer life, and it will no longer be a problem to abandon destructiveness. For one cannot succeed by forcing with the surface will, without a deep comprehension of the forces within that are the components of this very destructiveness. Yes, the will must of course be there in principle, but at the same time, as I have said in so many other contexts, the outer will should only be used for the purpose of liberating the inner powers that make the development a natural, organic, harmonious process. Thus destructiveness dissolves itself. It is not deliberately dropped like a cloak, nor are constructive feelings produced by a similar act of will. It is an evolutionary process within yourself, right here and now.

Another area where man finds himself extremely blocked, hindered and impatient with his own evolution or development is in connection with envy. This is a much more important topic than most of you realize. Here again, a number of my friends have begun to see that wherever their life is problematic, envy exists. Wherever there is no problem, they are free from it. Envy gives rise to self-hatred and to running away from that point within the envy which has to be transcended in order really and truly to come out of the envy-current and reconvert it to its original nature.

What causes envy is again the dualistic concept, in which life is understood in terms of either/or. "Either I have or the other has" is the nature of all envy. This implies the limitation with which man experiences the universe. The universe is infinite in its abundance and really knowing this makes envy impossible. What the other person has is not taken away from you. What you have was never taken away from another. The dualistic misconception presents innumerable problems. It not only creates envy, but also guilt; it paralyzes the relaxed powerful flow of reaching toward the good that can be yours. It makes you very hesitant to express and experience the best that is possible. It makes you see problems in a distorted fashion. It produces guilt for wanting and at the same time envying what others have.

This distorted perception of conditions in life is also responsible for an overall competitive attitude that afflicts mankind. This is manifest particularly strongly in some civilizations at certain periods of their history. Understanding the truth of the matter makes it impossible for one person to measure himself against another person. Comparison between two people is totally unrealistic; it measures two factors that cannot be measured. A specific strain is removed from the person who is no longer caught in this error. When you comprehend the unitive principle, that good is never divisible, a number of problems are eliminated. You will not be envious and therefore you will not feel guilty. You will not be faced with the apparent necessity of renouncing something in favor of someone else, because you will know deeply that what is yours is yours and what is the other person's is his. That very fact will make the selfishness and dishonesty existing in the childish nature, where the tendency to cheat life always prevails, impossible. You will not have to try to get away with anything, nor will you have to see yourself as special when you compare yourself with others.

We have discussed this topic before in connection with a question about the harm of the need to be special. In connection with the topic of this lecture, I say that this need is due to confusing the rightful tendency toward, and the inner need to bring about, full self-realization. What is the confusion here? Full self-realization always enhances the uniqueness of the individual. It does not level off individuality, nor does it imply mediocrity in the least—quite the contrary. Why, then, is it believed that not needing to be special means giving up individuality or even accepting mediocrity? The answer is that when the need to be special contains a desire to triumph over others, it signifies an attitude of being against others. It implies that self-enhancement can only exist at the expense of others. This is the either/or resulting from erroneous dualistic concepts, which are always destructive. It actually does destroy the other's value, at least in terms of your desire and aim, if not in actual fact. The further consequence is that the deep-seated self-regulating process of conscience says no to this endeavor and stops the outgoing energy current. This current then becomes either negative or numbed. This means that one is either passive, is paralyzed and holds back, or is ruthless, with the inevitable guilt and outer consequences.

The truth of the matter and the solution to this confusion can only be found when you distinguish between two totally different ways of measuring or evaluating—which lead to two totally different goals. When you want to be special in order to triumph over others, when your uniqueness exists at the expense of others and measures itself against others, this uniqueness is destructive and must lead to innumerable problems. But when you realize that your own specialness can be unlocked without measuring yourself against others, you will have no problem whatsoever. You will be free to unblock and unfold the best in yourself without infringing upon other people's rights or needs. Quite the contrary, your best will contribute to others rather than take away from them and you will give your best without the need to cheat, to get by, to get more than you give. The freedom of the power will activate more power. There will be no need to put the brakes on. Envy, guilt, dishonesty, and the belittling of others create the need to put the brakes on one's most constructive outgoing power current.

When man is ignorant of the fact that he has within himself the possibilities for self-fulfillment, the only way he can conceive of expressing himself is by measuring and comparing himself with others. When he knows that regardless of whether he is better or worse than others, he has his own quota of growth to fulfill for himself, he will not have any conflict about this subject. Of course you should give your best, but if in any way, no matter how secretly, your best is designed to lord it over others or to get special unfair privileges, to obtain something for nothing, you will get yourself in trouble. Then individuality cannot unfold because ego, vanity and ruthlessness take its place, and automatically hinder the positive power at work and convert it into destructive power.

When you feel envy or, on the other side of the same coin, the need to impress others or be better than they, try to feel the constructive power behind this need. For this need is only a distortion of the inborn urge to realize the best in you. When you do this, you will no longer find yourself blocked and paralyzed.

Are there any questions?

QUESTION: What makes the perception of pleasure so unique and specific in relation to the unpleasure?

ANSWER: This is a very important question and the answer may not seem to be a direct one, but it is. It is known that man fears pleasure when he is still full of conflicts and problems the nature of which he does not understand. Anyone on this path who goes deeply enough to probe his reactions discovers this startling fact: he is more afraid of pleasure than of pain. He who has not verified this fact in himself may find it unbelievable, for he consciously resents the unpleasure and wishes it away. And to a degree, this is right, for the unpleasure cannot really be wanted. Man cannot decipher this paradox when he does not go deep enough to feel the pleasure in the unpleasure within his psychic processes.

Total pleasure is feared for a very important reason: the pleasure supreme of the cosmic energy current must seem unbearable, too much, frightening, almost annihilating when the personality is still geared to negativity and destructiveness. To put it differently, to the degree that the personality has impaired its integrity, to the degree that impurity, dishonesty, cheating and malice exist in the psyche, pure pleasure must be rejected, so that the pain of the negative pleasure principle is the only way the entity can experience even a modicum of pleasure. When you, on your path, find that deep within yourself you fear pleasure as a danger, you must ask yourself, "Where am I not honest with life, with myself? Where do I cheat? Where do I impair my integrity?" This is precisely where, why, and to what degree pure pleasure must be rejected. When man ascertains in himself that he fears and rejects pleasure, rather than being deprived of it by life, he can do something by asking himself the pertinent questions and subsequently finding the elements of impairment in himself. This is the way out. When he finds where he violates his sense of decency and honesty, he can unlock the door which prevents him from transforming the negative pleasure and which forces him to reject pleasure that is unhampered by pain.

QUESTION: Would you define pleasure as expansion and pain as contraction?

ANSWER: Yes, that is quite true. Pain is a contraction in the sense of a cramp. But there is also contraction in pure pleasure—only in a rhythmic smooth motion, in a harmonious way. Unpleasure is an extended, protracted contraction, in a cramp-like fashion.

QUESTION: The way I experience fear of pleasure is by experiencing a fear of losing myself in pleasure. Is that what you meant?

ANSWER: Yes, this is precisely what I meant. This can be explained when you think about it in terms of trust. When you consciously or unconsciously sense deeply the hidden little mechanisms by which you avoid being straightforward with the life process, when your response to life is negative in any form and consequently your sense of integrity is impaired, you cannot trust yourself. Nor can you trust yourself when you run away from the nucleus of your negative pleasure principle, as explained in this lecture. It has to be accepted, understood and inwardly lived through in full self-acceptance before you can trust yourself to be unguarded.

As I have often said, your innermost self, your own psychic energies and the life energies are of one and the same substance; you cannot trust yourself without trusting life. If you distrust yourself on some level for any reason—right or wrong—how can you lose yourself into yourself and into life? A trust must exist and this trust is, in principle, absolutely justifiable. But in practice, in specific manifestations, it is often not justifiable. Full self-acceptance must be established before trust can exist. Then there will no longer be any fear of losing yourself, because such loss of self will be experienced as bringing you back to yourself, richer than ever.

QUESTION: Is the principle of pain and pleasure characteristic of this earth sphere?

ANSWER: It is characteristic of this earth sphere, but this does not merely mean incarnated beings. It means all those who are in this specific state of consciousness, whether they are in the flesh or out of the body. It applies to all those whose consciousness is geared to the concept of dualism, who cannot perceive the conciliating, unifying way of creation, of life, of themselves. In all these cases, pleasure and pain must exist as opposites. As I said at the beginning of this lecture, the good and the bad forces, pleasure and pain, are thought of as two separate forces, not one and the same energy current.

QUESTION: It seems to me that when I do something I don't like, which is meant to invite anger or guilt or jealousy, that I have someone else whom I hold responsible for my being the way I am. Is this a valid observation and what should we do about it?

ANSWER: Even if some of the blame is rightfully put on the other person's doorstep—and this is usually the case with sane human beings—there must be something in you that you ignore and which bothers you, for otherwise there could be no problem, no disharmonious feeling in you. It would be relatively easy to accept the other person's shortcomings or failings. Otherwise one would not be involved in situations where these failings cannot help but negatively affect the self. The very existence of such disturbances points to unknown elements which must be ascertained in order to eliminate destructive feelings. Hence this anger is essentially directed against the self. You may be angry because you are angry and you cannot accept this emotion in yourself. You may become angry because you cannot accept a similar or corresponding aspect in yourself. That is, that which angers you in the other may exist in a slightly different form in yourself. In short, this question must be asked: "What is it in me that has produced this situation? How am I a co-producer of this situation? In what way do I contribute to it?"

Again, the dualistic concept of life hinders and confuses. If one attempts to solve such a problem in an attitude of finding either the one or the other person at fault, no solution exists. Neither of these two alternatives satisfies, for each must be off the mark or superficial in evaluation. True enlightenment can only come when the unconscious interaction, how one's inner problem affects the other person's inner problem, is seen as interacting vicious circles. When you truly realize that the situation must be a co-production, then you can begin to make serious headway in the right direction.

The second thing I have to say here is that often a person cannot find the answer because he looks for the cause in a limited or moralistic way. The way he has contributed to the situation may be altogether different from what he feels defensive about. For example, a person tries to exonerate himself because he senses a badness in himself. Actually his contribution may not be anything bad or mean at all. It may be rather that he underestimates his values, his rights, his entire person. He may be weak, submissive, not assertive enough and thus encourages a negative situation in a very different way from that which he vaguely defends against in himself. Such weakness is always a result of some disturbance of the psyche on a deep level and cannot help but create negativity and destructiveness, but the way to eliminate it is not by forcing the destructive feelings away. This cannot succeed. One must work on a very deep level with these problems. Often weakness is confused with goodness, and strength with ruthlessness or selfishness. In these confusions, man does not find the way to resolve the problem and find clarity.

Therefore, I suggest a meditation that reaches deep into the self: "I do want to see where I possibly violate some spiritual law, where I am wrong in the usual sense of the word, but I would also like to know where I am weak and confused and because of it, negative emotions come into existence. Where is it that I am perhaps not aware of my values and because of this lack of awareness, I fight in the wrong way? I would like to see these elements and straighten them out. I want to see both these aspects." Usually they interact; they are not unconnected elements. Lack of self-assertion on one level may induce an angry overassertion on the surface. When the meditation is directed into such channels, new vision may come— vision that was hitherto blocked.

May your understanding grow so that you sense your own distortions and how these distortions are a valuable life energy that can be activated in the specific way I showed here.

Be blessed, every one of you; receive the strength and the power that flows into you. Make use of it, travel this path to the very nucleus of your own inner being. Be in God!

Compulsion to Recreate and Overcome Childhood Hurts

R E E T I N G S, my dearest friends. God bless all of you. May the divine blessings extended to everyone of you help you assimilate the words I speak tonight, so that this will be a fruitful evening for you.

Our last discussion was about the fear of loving. The subject of love was presented at great length and from various angles in past sessions. You will remember that I frequently mentioned how the child desires to be loved exclusively and without limit. In other words, the child's desire to be loved is unrealistic. Yet it is also true that the child would be very satisfied with real mature love. In fact, if it were given, the unrealistic demand for exclusive love would be diminished considerably. However, the capacity for tendering genuine mature love is rare indeed.

Since the child so seldom receives sufficient mature love and warmth, he continues to hunger for it throughout life unless this lack and hurt is recognized and properly dealt with. If not, the person will go through life unconsciously crying out for what he missed in childhood. This will cause an inability to love maturely. You can see how this condition spreads from generation to generation.

The remedy cannot be found by wishing that things were different and that people would learn to practice mature love. The remedy lies solely in you. True, if you had received this love from your parents, you would be without this unconscious problem—a problem of which you are not really and fully aware. But this lack need not trouble you nor your life if you see it, become aware of it, and rearrange your former unconscious wishes, regrets, thoughts, and concepts. As a consequence, you will not only become a happier person, but you will also be able to extend mature love to others—your children, if you have any, or to other people—so that a benign chain reaction is started. This is contrary to your present inner behavior, which we shall now consider.

This unconscious problem is greatly overlooked by all humanity and even by the few who have started to explore their own unconscious mind and emotions. Very few people realize and personally experience—theoretical knowledge notwithstanding—the strong link between the child's longing and unfulfillment and the adult's present difficulties and problems. It is very important to become aware of this link.

There may be isolated, exceptional cases where one parent offers a sufficient degree of mature love. Even if one parent offers it to some degree, very likely the other does not. Since mature love on this earth is only a question of degree, the child will suffer from the shortcomings of even a loving parent.

More often, however, both parents are emotionally immature and cannot give the love the child craves, or only in insufficient measure. During childhood, this need is rarely conscious. The child has no way of putting his need into thoughts. He cannot compare. He does not know that something else might exist. He believes this is the way it should be. Or, in extreme cases, he feels especially isolated, believing his lot is like no one else's. Both attitudes are not according to truth. In both cases, the true emotion is not conscious and therefore is not properly evaluated and accepted. Thus, the child grows up never quite understanding why he is unhappy, or even that he is unhappy. Many of you look back on childhood convinced that you had all the love you wanted just because you actually did have some love, but rarely all that you wanted.

There are a number of parents who give great demonstrations of love. They may spoil or pamper their children. This very act of spoiling and pampering may be an overcompensation and something like an apology for a deeply suspected inability to love maturely. The child feels the truth very acutely. He may not think it, he may not consciously observe it, but inwardly the child keenly feels the difference between mature, genuine love and immature over-demonstration offered instead of it.

Proper guidance and security are a parent's responsibility and call for authority on his part. There is the parent who never dares to punish or exert such a healthy authority. This is due to guilt because real, giving, warming, comforting love is absent in his own immature personality. Another parent may be too severe, too strict. He thereby exerts a distortion of authority by bullying and not allowing the individuality of the child to unfold. Both fall short as parents, and their wrong attitudes will be absorbed by the child and will result in hurt and unfulfillment.

In the case of the strict parent, the resentment and rebellion will be open and therefore more easily traced. In the other case, the rebellion is just as strong, but hidden and therefore infinitely harder to trace. If you had a parent who smothered you with affection or pseudo-affection, yet lacked in genuine warmth or if you had a parent who conscientiously did everything right, but also was lacking in real warmth, unconsciously you knew it when you were a child and you resented it. Consciously, you may not be aware of it at all because, when a child, you really could not put your finger on the lack. You were outwardly given everything you wanted and needed. How could you make the subtle borderline distinction between real affection and pseudo-affection in your intellect? The fact that something bothered you without your being able to explain it reasonably made you feel guilty and uncomfortable. You therefore pushed it out of sight as much as possible.

As long as this hurt, disappointment, and unfulfilled need from your early years is unconscious, you cannot come to terms with it. No matter how much you may love your parents, unconscious resentment exists and therefore you cannot forgive them for the hurt. You can only forgive and let go if you recognize this deeply hidden hurt and resentment. As an adult human being, you will see that your parents too are just human beings. They were not as faultless and perfect as the child thought and hoped and are not to be rejected because they had their own conflicts and immaturities. The light of conscious reasoning has to be applied to the very emotions you never allowed yourself to be aware of fully.

As long as you are unaware of this conflict, of your longing for perfect love from your parents, you are bound to try remedying the situation in your later years. This may manifest in various aspects of your life. You run into problems and repeated patterns which have their origin in your attempt to reproduce the childhood situation so as to correct it. This unconscious compulsion is a very strong factor, but is so deeply hidden from your conscious understanding!

The most frequent way of attempting to remedy the situation is in your choice of love partners. Unconsciously, you will know how to choose in the partner aspects of the parent who has particularly fallen short in affection and love that is real and genuine. But you also seek in your partner aspects of the other parent who has come closer to meeting your needs. Important as it is to find both parents represented in your partners, it is even more important and more difficult to find those aspects which represent the parent who has particularly disappointed and hurt you, the one more resented or despised and for whom you had little or no love. So you seek the parents again—in a subtle way that is not always easy to detect—in your marital partners, in your friendships, or in other human relationships. In your subconscious, the following reactions take place: since the child in you cannot let go of the past, cannot come to terms with it, cannot forgive, cannot understand and accept, this child in you always creates similar conditions, trying to win out in the end, to finally master the situation instead of succumbing. Losing out means being crushed and this must be avoided at all cost. The costs are high, indeed, for the entire process is unfeasible. What the child in you sets out to accomplish cannot ever come to realization.

This entire procedure is utterly destructive. In the first place, it is an illusion that you were defeated. Therefore, it is an illusion that you can be victorious. Moreover, it is an illusion that the lack of love, sad as that may have been when you were a child, is as great a tragedy as your subconscious still feels it to be. The only tragedy lies in the fact that you obstruct your future happiness by continuing to reproduce and then attempting to master the situation. It goes without saying, my friends, that this process is unconscious. Of course, nothing is further from your mind in your conscious aims and wishes. It will take a great deal of digging to uncover the emotions that lead you again and again into situations in which your secret aim is to remedy childhood woes.

In trying to reproduce the childhood situation, you unconsciously choose a partner with aspects similar to those of the parent. These very aspects will make it as impossible to receive the mature love you rightfully long for now as it was then. Blindly you believe that by willing it more strongly and more forcefully, the parent-partner will now yield, whereas in reality, love cannot come that way. Free of this ever continuing repetition, you will no longer cry to be loved by the parent. Instead, you will look for a partner, or other human relationships, with the aim of finding the maturity you really need and want. In not demanding to be loved as a child, you will be equally willing to love. However, the child in you finds this impossible, no matter how much you may otherwise be capable of it through development and progress. This hidden conflict eclipses your otherwise growing soul.

If you already have a partner, the uncovering of this conflict may show you his or her immaturities and similarities to your parents. But, as you know, totally mature people hardly exist. Once this is accepted, such immaturities will no longer seem as tragic as they did when you were blindly searching to find your parent or parents again. With your existing immaturities and inabilities, you may nevertheless build a more mature relationship, free of the childish compulsion now under discussion.

You have no idea how preoccupied your subconscious is with the process of reenacting the play, so to speak, only hoping that "this time it will be different." And it never is! As time goes on, each disappointment weighs heavier and your soul becomes more discouraged.

For those of my friends who have not yet reached certain depths of their unexplored subconscious, this may sound quite preposterous and contrived. But those of you who have come to see the power of your hidden trends, compulsions and images, will not only readily believe it, but you will soon experience the truth of these words in your own personal life. You already know from other findings how potent is the working of your subconscious, how shrewdly it goes about its destructive and illogical way.

If you learn to look at your problems and unfulfillment from this point of view, and by the usual process allow your emotions to come to the fore, you will gain much further insight. But it will be necessary, my friends, to re-experience the longing and the hurt of the crying child that once you were, even though you were also a happy one. Your happiness may have been valid and without self-deception at all, for it is possible to be both happy and unhappy. You may be perfectly aware of the happy aspects of your childhood, but that which hurt deeply and that certain something you greatly longed for—you did not even quite know what—you were not aware of. You took the situation for granted. You did not know what was missing or that there was something missing. This basic unhappiness has to come to awareness now, if you really want to proceed in inner growth. You have to re-experience the acute pain you once suffered but you pushed out of sight. Now this pain has to be looked at with the understanding you have gained. Only by doing this will you understand the reality-value of your current problems and see them in their true light.

Now, how can you manage to re-experience the hurts of so long ago? There is only one way, my friends. Take a current problem. Strip if of all the superimposed layers of your reactions. The first and most handy layer is that of rationalization, that of "proving" that others, or situations are at fault, not your innermost conflicts which make you adopt the wrong attitude to the actual problem that confronts you. The next layer might be anger, resentment, anxiety, frustration. Behind all these reactions, you will find the hurt of not being loved. We went into this thoroughly in a previous lecture. When you experience the hurt of not being loved in your current dilemma, it will serve to re-awaken the childhood hurt. With the present hurt, think back, try to re-evaluate the situation as to your parents. What they gave you, how you really felt about them. You will become aware that in many ways you lacked something you never clearly saw before—you did not want to see it. You will find that this must have hurt you when you were a child, but you may have forgotten this hurt on a conscious level. Yet it is not forgotten at all. The hurt of your current problem is the very same hurt. Now re-evaluate your present hurt, comparing it with the childhood hurt. Finally, you will clearly see how it is one and the same. No matter how true and understandable your present pain is, it is nevertheless the same childhood pain. A little later, you will see how you contributed to bringing about the present pain because of your desire to correct the childhood hurt. But, at first, you only have to feel the similarity of the pain. This however requires considerable effort, for there are so many overlaying emotions that cover the present pain as well as the past one. Before you have succeeded in crystallizing the pain, you cannot understand anything further in this respect.

Once you can synchronize these two pains and realize that they are one and the same, the next step will be much easier. Then, by looking over the repetitious pattern in your various problems you will learn to recognize where the similarities exist in your parents and in the people who have caused you hurt or are causing you pain now. When you experience these similarities emotionally, it will carry you further on the particular road toward dissolving this basic problem. Mere intellectual evaluation will not yield any benefit. When you feel the similarities, while at the same time experiencing the pain of now and the pain of then, you will slowly come to understand how you thought you had to choose the current situation because deep inside you could not possibly admit "defeat."

It goes without saying that many people are not even aware of any pain, past or present. They busily push it out of sight. Their problems do not appear as "pain." For them, the very first step is to become aware that this pain is present and that it hurts infinitely more as long as they have not become aware of it. Many people are afraid of this pain and like to believe that ignoring it means it is not there. They choose such a path only because their conflicts become too great for them. How much more wonderful it is for a person to choose this path in the wisdom and conviction that a hidden conflict, in the long run, does as much damage as a manifest one. They will not fear to uncover the real emotion and will feel, even in the temporary experience of acute pain, that in that moment it turns into a healthy growing pain, free of bitterness, tension, anxiety, and frustration.

There are also those who tolerate the pain but in a negative way, always expecting it to be remedied from the outside. In a way such people are nearer to the solution, because for them it will be quite easy to see how the childish process still operates. "The outside" is the offending parent, or both parents, projected onto other human beings. They have only to redirect the approach to their pain. They do not have to find it.

Only after experiencing all these emotions, and synchronizing the "now" and the "then," will you become aware of how you tried to correct the situation. You will further see the folly of this unconscious desire, the frustrating uselessness of it. You will survey all your actions and reactions with this new understanding and insight, whereupon you will release your parents, you will leave your childhood truly behind and start a new inner behavior pattern that will be infinitely more constructive and rewarding for you and for others. You will no longer seek to master the situation that you could not master as a child. You will go on from where you are, forgetting and forgiving truly inside of you without thinking that you have done so. You will no longer need to be loved as you needed to be loved when you were a child. First, you become aware that this is what you still wish, and then you no longer seek this type of love. Since you are no longer a child, you will seek love in a different way, by giving it instead of by expecting it. But it must always be emphasized that many people are not aware that they do expect it. Since the childish, unconscious expectation was so often disappointed, they made themselves give up all expectations and all desire for love. Needless to say, this is neither genuine nor healthy, for it is a wrong extreme.

To be fruitful and bring real results, this must go beyond mere intellectual knowledge. You have to allow yourself to feel the pain of certain unfulfillments now and also the pain of the unfulfillment of your childhood. Then compare the two until, like two separate picture slides, they gradually move into focus and become one. Once this happens, the insight that you gain, the experience that you feel exactly as I say here, will enable you to take the further steps indicated.

All this is of great importance for some of my friends who are well enough advanced in their own work. They need this instruction to give them a new outlook, to gain further clarification beyond the point at which they have arrived and enable them to proceed in the proper direction. For others who are not yet that far advanced or for new friends in the group who have not really begun a self-search, these words may perhaps be a little obscure. They may understand quite well intellectually, but they will be unable as yet to apply them to their own emotions and life-problems. Nevertheless, I say to all these friends: think about it, the time will come when you will glean a new understanding about yourself from these words. Perhaps an occasional glimpse even now, a temporary flickering emotion that these words may cause in you will be of help and open a door toward knowing yourself better, toward evaluating your life with a more realistic, more mature outlook.

Now, are there any questions in connection with this lecture?

QUESTION: There is something very difficult for me to understand here. One continuously chooses a person, a love-object, who has exactly the same negative traits that one or the other parent had; is it in reality that this particular person has these traits, or is it projection and response?

ANSWER: It can be both and it can be either. In fact, most of the time it is a combination. Certain aspects are unconsciously looked for and found and they are actually, in reality, similarities. But these existing similarities are enhanced by the person. They are not projected—qualities "seen" that are not really there—but these qualities are latent to some degree without being manifested. These are encouraged and strongly brought to the fore by the attitude of the person with his unrecognized inner

problem. In other words, you—I do not mean you personally—foster something in the other person by provoking him
or her to react that way. The provocation, which of course is
entirely unconscious, is a very strong factor here.

This sum total of a human personality consists of many aspects. Out of these, let us say three or four are actually similar.
The most outstanding factor would be a similar kind of immaturity and incapacity to love as in the parent in question.
That alone is sufficient and potent enough in essence to reproduce the same situation.

The same person would not react with others as he reacts
with you because it is you who provoke him constantly into
reproducing similar conditions for you to correct. Your fear,
your self-punishment, your frustration, your anger, your hostility, your withdrawal from giving out love and affection, all
these behaviors and attitudes of the child in you constantly
provoke the other person and enhance in him that which is
weak and immature. The more mature person, however, will
affect others differently and will bring out that in them which
is mature and whole, for there is no person who does not have
some mature aspects.

QUESTION: You have stated that emotional maturity is the willingness
and the capability to love. It seems to me that intellectual maturity must mean something else. How do the two interplay
and influence each other?

ANSWER: Both are necessary functions of the healthy individual. As
I once put it, they are like the two legs you need in order to
walk through life. Intellectual maturity is your capacity to
think, to judge, to evaluate, to discriminate, to form concepts, to plan, to use your will, to use your mind, to make
decisions, to utilize your assets, to direct your life and, last
but not least, to educate, or re-educate the childish emotions
by implanting the proper concepts—your own—that you
have arrived at independently by thinking things through.
Not because others said so, but because you deliberated on
them are they your own. Thus, your intellect can influence
your emotions by your capacity to think. On the other hand,

unchecked and childish emotions can influence your thinking capacity by coloring your views, by making you lose objectivity. Your capacity to think is intellectual maturity. And the way you manage your emotional reactions, feelings, and instincts determines your emotional maturity or lack of it.

QUESTION: How can I make the distinction as to whether the other person provoked me or I the other person?

ANSWER: It is not necessary to find who started it for this is a chain reaction, a vicious circle. It is useful to start by finding your own provocation, perhaps in response to an open—or hidden—provocation of the other person. Thus you realize that because you were provoked, you provoke the other person. And because you do so, the other again responds in kind. But as you examine your real reason, not the superficial one, why you were hurt in the first place and therefore provoked, in the sense of tonight's lecture, you will no longer regard this hurt as disastrous, as it appeared before. You will have a different reaction to the hurt, and as a consequence the hurt will diminish automatically. Therefore, you will no longer feel the need to provoke the other person. Also, as the need to reproduce the childhood situation decreases, you will become less withdrawn and you will hurt others less and less so that they will not have to provoke you. And if they do, you will understand also that they reacted out of the same childish blind needs as you do. As you gain a different view of your own hurt, understanding its real origin, you will gain the same detachment to the reaction of the other person. You will find exactly the same reactions going on in you and the other. But so long as that conflict remains unsolved in you, the difference seems enormous. You ascribe different motivation to the other person's provocation than to your own, even if and when you actually realize that you initiated the provocation. Thus you perceive reality while before you did not, and so you begin to break this vicious circle.

As you truly perceive the mutual interplay, it will relieve the feeling of isolation and guilt you all are burdened with. You are constantly fluctuating between your guilt and the accusation of injustice directed at those around you. The child in you feels itself entirely different, in a world of its own. That is such a damaging illusion. As you solve this conflict, it will increase your awareness of other people—you are so unaware of the reality of other people. On the one hand, you accuse them and are inordinately hurt by them because you do not understand yourself and therefore do not understand the other person. On the other hand and at the same time, you refuse to become aware when you are hurt. This seems paradoxical yet is not. As you experience for yourself the factors set forth tonight, you will find this to be true. While some times you may exaggerate a hurt, at other times you do not allow yourself to know it happened at all because it may not fit the picture you have for the situation. It may spoil your constructed idea. It may not correspond to your desire at the time. If otherwise the situation seems favorable and fits into your preconceived idea, you leave out all that jars you, while it festers underneath and creates unconscious hostility. This entire reaction inhibits your intuitive faculties, at least in this particular respect.

The constant provocation among human beings, hidden from your awareness now, is a reality you will come to perceive very clearly. This will have a very liberating effect on you and your surroundings. But you cannot perceive it unless you understand the factors in yourself I discussed tonight.

QUESTION: Is it possible in some way to make a truce, for even two or three minutes, between one's own subconscious and the subconscious of the other person? Sometimes you see the reality intellectually, but by the time you order your subconscious to do something, it is already in revolt and has made the other person unhappy and then you are unhappy too. It might all have been avoided if there were a few minutes of truce.

ANSWER: You see my dear, in the first place, it is not a question of ordering your subconscious; you cannot order it. That is impossible. As long as you attempt such commands, it will be very resistant. Or it may deceive you, so that you deceive yourself. The subconscious can only be re-educated by the slow and gradual process we pursue in our work. Most important is that you become fully aware of what you really feel. Actually, you are only half aware of it most of the time and resort to superimposing another set of feelings upon your real reactions. These may be other negative emotions, or, if positive, you are deceiving yourself even more. Only by stripping away all these superimpositions can you understand the reason why your subconscious is often so stubborn. If it continues to resist your good efforts, there must be something present that you have not understood and connected. Then it is a question of finding the block causing this particular obstruction. When this happens, you will not need a short truce. You will have real peace with yourself and therefore with others. While you may command a truce in your outer actions, your words, and even your thoughts, the subconscious does not respond to such discipline. It goes on in its own way until it has really changed.

A truce, as you see it, cannot really work. It is as unreal as would be the effect of attempting to command it.

QUESTION: Suppose a person is able to put his house in order. Will he then eliminate provocations in the other person?

ANSWER: You do not even have to put your house in order to the extent that you are fully mature and more or less perfect. This perfection hardly ever exists in the human sphere. But the awareness of your immaturity, real insight into and understanding of your reactions and feelings that cause provocation, will weaken it sufficiently until you finally cease bringing on provocations and you in turn will not be provoked by others. As you gain a certain detachment from yourself in a healthy way, the smoldering, unhealthy drive, the force is taken out of your emotional reactions. In fact, I would even say that this is the only kind of valid "truce" that can be accomplished. Allow yourself to see what you really feel and why. And when you have an overall view without any further subterfuge and self-deception, such knowledge will no longer disquiet you. It will have a calming effect. You will have made peace with yourself by accepting your still existing imperfections and will no longer harrow yourself into trying for a perfection that you cannot possibly attain at the moment. Once you accept the reality of your imperfect self, the resulting hurts will no longer be so serious and tragic. You will accept them as a consequence of your accepted imperfections which you can now observe calmly, while gaining more understanding about them and thus nearing perfection and maturity. In this way, your hostility will vanish and your provocations as well. Relapses will surely occur, but you will accept them with a realistic outlook. You will gain further insight from them, knowing that if they are possible, it is because something has not penetrated deeply enough and has to be found anew so as to be assimilated on deeper levels of your being.

Hostility exists because you are unaware that you are hurt and why you are hurt. Just think of times when you are really aware of a hurt without anger, and without feeling hostile. You may feel sad, but feeling sad seems to many people so humiliating that they prefer to be angry and therefore hostile. That is a particular kind of childishness existing in everyone. You think it is superior to be angry and hostile than to be sad, so you suppress the real hurt. But the hostility has to be hidden too because it makes you feel guilty for other reasons, so that it comes out in a devious, hidden way, which in turn brings on further provocation. Provocation is a result of unaware hostility, suppressed hostility, and the hostility results from unaware and suppressed hurt.

Go your way, my dearest ones, and may the blessings we bring all of you envelop and penetrate your body, soul, and spirit, so that you open up your soul and become your real self, your own real self. Be blessed, my friends, be in peace, be in God!

The Forces of
Love, Eros
and Sex

G R E E T I N G S in the Name of the Lord. I bring you blessings, my dearest friends. Blessed is this hour.

Tonight I should like to discuss three particular forces in the universe: the love force, as it manifests between the sexes; the erotic force; and the sex force. These are three distinctly different principles or forces that manifest differently on each plane, from the highest to the lowest. Humanity has always confused these three principles. In fact, it is little known that these three separate forces exist and what the differences among them are. There is so much confusion about this that it should be most useful for my friends to hear how it is in reality.

The sex force is the creative force on any level of existence. In the highest spheres, the same sex force creates spiritual life, spiritual ideas, spiritual concepts and principles, as it does on your earth sphere. But on the lower planes the unspiritualized sex force creates life as it manifests in that particular sphere: it creates the outer shell or vehicle of the entity destined to live in that sphere.

The erotic force is one of the most potent forces in existence and has tremendous momentum and impact. It is supposed to serve as the bridge between sex and love, yet it rarely does. In a spiritually highly developed person, the erotic force carries the entity from the erotic experience, which itself is of short duration, into the permanent state of love. However, even the strong momentum of the erotic force carries the soul just so far and no farther. It is bound to dissolve if the personality does not know how to love, if he or she does not cultivate all the qualities and requirements necessary for true love; once he or she does, the spark of the erotic force will remain alive. By itself, without love, the erotic force burns itself out. This of course is the trouble with marriage. Since most people are incapable of pure love, they are also incapable of ideal marriage.

Eros in many ways seems similar to love. It brings forth in a human being impulses that he otherwise would not have: impulses of unselfishness and affection he might have been incapable of before. This is why eros is so very often confused with love. It is just as often confused with the sex instinct which, like eros, also manifests as a great urge.

Now my friends, I would like to show you what the spiritual meaning and purpose of the erotic force is, particularly as far as humanity is concerned. Without eros, many people would never experience the great feeling and beauty that is contained in real love. They would never get the taste of it, and the yearning for love would remain deeply submerged in their souls. Their fear of love would remain the stronger urge.

Eros is the nearest thing to love the undeveloped spirit can experience. It lifts the soul out of sluggishness, out of mere contentment and vegetation. It causes the soul to surge, to go out of itself. When this force comes upon even the most undeveloped person, he will become able to surpass himself. Even a delinquent will temporarily feel, at least toward the one person, a goodness he has never known. The utterly selfish person will, while this feeling lasts, have unselfish impulses. The lazy person will get out of his inertia. The routine-bound person will naturally and without great effort get rid of his static habits. The erotic force will lift the person out of his separateness, be it only for a short time. This gives the soul a foretaste of unity and teaches the fear-filled psyche the longing for it. This longing becomes more conscious because of the erotic experience. The more strongly one has experienced it, the less contentment the soul will find in the pseudo-security of separateness. During the experience of eros, an otherwise thoroughly self-centered person may even be able to make a sacrifice. So you see, my friends, eros enables persons to do many things that they are disinclined to do otherwise; things that are closely linked with love. It is easy to see why eros is so often confused with love.

How then, is it different from love? Love is a permanent state in the soul. Love can exist only if the foundation for it is prepared through development and purification. Love does not come and go at random; eros does.

Eros hits with a sudden force, often taking a person unawares, and even finding him unwilling to go through the experience. Only if the soul is prepared to love and has built the foundation for it will eros be the bridge to the love that is manifest between a man and a woman.

Thus you can see how important the erotic force is. Without the erotic force "hitting" him and getting him out of the rut, many a human being would never be lifted out of himself, would never see beyond himself, would never be ready for a more conscious search for some means of breaking down his own wall of separation. The erotic experience puts the seed into the soul and makes it long for unity which is the great aim in the Plan. As long as the soul is separate, loneliness and unhappiness must be the result. The erotic experience enables the personality to long for union with at least one other being. In the heights of the spirit world, union exists among all beings—and thus with God. In the earth sphere, the erotic force is in itself a propelling power, regardless of whether or not its real meaning is understood. This is so even though it is often misused and enjoyed—while it lasts—for its own sake and not utilized to cultivate love in the soul, in which case it peters out. Nevertheless, the effect will inevitably remain in the soul.

Eros suddenly comes to man in certain stages of his life, even to those who are afraid of the apparent risk of the adventure away from separateness. He who is afraid of his emotions and afraid of life as such will often do anything in his power (subconsciously and ignorantly) to avoid the great experience of unity. Although this fear exists in many, many human beings, there are few indeed who have not experienced some opening in the soul where eros can touch them. For the fear-ridden soul that resists the experience, this is good medicine, regardless of the fact that sorrow and loss may follow due to other psychological factors too varied to enumerate now.

However, there are also those who are over-emotional, and although they may know other fears of life, they are not afraid of this particular experience. In fact, the beauty of it is a great temptation to them and therefore they hunt greedily for it. They look for one subject after another. They are unwilling to learn pure love; they simply use the erotic force for their pleasure and when it is worn out, they hunt elsewhere. This of course is abuse and cannot continue without ill effect. This type of personality will have to make up for the abuse—ignorant as it may have been—just as the over-fearful coward will have to make up for trying to cheat life by hiding from it and thus withholding from the soul a medicine that is valuable if used properly. As I have said, somewhere in the soul there is a vulnerable point for most people in this category through which eros can enter.

There are also a few who have built such a tight wall of fear and pride around their souls that they avoid this part of the life-experience entirely and so cheat their own development. This fear might exist because, in a former life, unhappiness resulted from this life experience, or perhaps because the soul has greedily abused the beauty of it without building it into love. In both cases the personality may have chosen to be more careful. If this decision is too rigid, the opposite extreme will follow. In the next incarnation circumstances will be chosen in such a way that a balance is established until the soul reaches a harmonious state wherein no more extremes exist. This applies to all aspects of the personality, as well as to this particular subject.

In order to approach this harmony to some extent at least, the proper balance between reason, emotion and will has to be achieved in the personality.

The erotic experience often mingles with the sexual urge, but it does not always have to be that way. These three forces—love, eros and sex—often appear completely separately, while sometimes two mingle, let us say eros and sex, or eros and love, as much as the soul is capable of love, or sex and a semblance of love. Only in the ideal case do all three forces mingle harmoniously.

The pure sex force is utterly selfish. Where sex exists without eros and without love, it is referred to as "animalistic." Pure sex exists in all living creatures: animals, plants and minerals. Eros begins with the stage of development where the soul is incarnated as a human being. And pure love is to be found in the higher spiritual realms. This does not mean that eros and sex no longer exist in beings of higher development, but rather that all three blend harmoniously, are refined, and become less and less selfish. This does not mean that a human being cannot try for this harmonious blend of all three forces.

In rare cases, eros alone, without sex and love, exists for a limited time. This is usually referred to as "platonic love." But sooner or later with the somewhat healthy person, eros and sex will mingle. The sex force, instead of being suppressed, is taken up, so to speak, by the erotic force and both flow in one current. The more these three forces remain separate, the more unhealthy the personality is.

Another possibility, particularly in relationships of long standing, is the combination of a certain kind of love (it cannot be perfect unless all three forces blend together, but let us say, the nearest to perfect love) and sex but without eros. There is a certain amount of affection, companionship, fondness, mutual respect and a sex relationship that is crudely sexual without the erotic spark, which evaporated some time ago. When eros is missing, the sex relationship must eventually suffer. Now this is the problem with most marriages, my friends. There is hardly a human being who is not puzzled by this question of what to do to maintain that spark in a relationship, which seems to evaporate as habit and knowledge of one another advance. You may not have thought of it in exactly this way, in terms of three distinct forces, yet you know and sense that something goes out of a marriage that was present at the beginning: that certain spark that is actually eros. You find yourself in a vicious circle and thus think that marriage is a hopeless proposition. No, my friends, it is not, even if you cannot as yet attain the ideal.

Let me now tell you about the ideal partnership of love between two people. I have already said that all three forces have to be represented. With love you do not seem to have much difficulty, for in most cases one would not marry if there did not exist at least the willingness to love. I will not discuss at this point the extreme cases where this is not so. I am discussing the case where the choice is a mature one and yet one cannot get around the pitfall of time and habit because elusive eros has disappeared.

With sex it is the same. The sex force is present in most healthy human beings and may only begin to fade (particularly with women) when eros has left. Men may then seek eros elsewhere. For the sexual relationship must eventually suffer when eros is not maintained. And how can you keep eros? This is the big question, my dear ones. Eros can be maintained only if it is used as a bridge to true partnership in love in the highest sense. We will now discuss how this is done.

Let us first see the main element in the erotic force. When you analyze it, you will find that it is the adventure, the search for knowledge of the other soul. This desire lives in every created spirit. This inherent life force must finally bring the entity out of its separation. Eros strengthens the curiosity to know the other being. As long as there is something new to find in the other soul and as long as you reveal yourself, eros will live. The moment you believe you have found all there is to find and have revealed all there is to reveal—or all you are willing to reveal—eros will leave. It is as simple as that with eros. But where your great error comes in is that you believe there is a limit to the revealing of any soul, yours or another's. When a certain point of usually quite superficial revelation is reached, one is under the impression that this is all there is, and settles down to a placid life without further searching.

Eros has carried you this far with its strong impact. But after this point, your will to further search the unlimited depths of the other person and voluntarily to reveal and share your own inward search determines whether you have used eros as a bridge to love. This in turn is always determined by your will to learn how to love. Only in this way will you maintain the spark of eros contained in your love. Only in this way will you continue to find the other and let yourself be found. There is no limit, for the soul is endless and eternal: a whole lifetime would not suffice to know it. There can never be a point, at any time, when you know the other soul entirely, nor when you are known entirely. The soul is alive and nothing that is alive remains static. It changes constantly. It has the capacity to reveal even deeper layers that already exist, apart from any change. The soul is in constant change and movement, as is anything spiritual, by its very nature. Spirit means life and life means change. Since soul is spirit, the soul can never be known utterly. If man had the wisdom, he would realize that, and make of marriage the marvelous journey of adventure it is supposed to be, forever finding new vistas, instead of merely being carried only as far as you are taken by the first momentum of eros. You should use this potent momentum of eros as the initial thrust it is, and then find through it the urge to go further "under your own steam." Then will you have brought eros into true love in marriage.

Marriage is meant by God for human beings and the divine purpose is not merely procreation. This is only one detail. The spiritual idea of marriage is to enable the soul to reveal itself and to be constantly on the search for the other, to discover forever and ever new vistas of the other being. The more this happens, the happier will the marriage be, the more firmly and safely will it be rooted, the less it will be in danger of an unhappy ending and the more does it fulfill its spiritual purpose.

In practice, however, it hardly ever works that way. You reach a certain state of familiarity and habit and you think you know the other and it does not even occur to you that the other does not know you at all. He or she may know certain facets of you, but that is all. This search for the other being, as well as for self-revelation requires a certain amount of inner activity and alertness. But since man is often tempted into inner inactivity, outer activity may become stronger as over-compensation. He is then tempted into a state of restfulness, under the illusion that he already knows the other fully. This is the pitfall. It is the beginning of the end at worst, and at best, a compromise with a gnawing, unfulfilled longing. At this point, the relationship begins to become static. It is no longer alive even though it may have some very pleasant facets. Habit is the great temptress, pulling one toward a sluggishness and inertia in which one does not have to try and work or be alert anymore.

Two people may arrange an apparently satisfactory relationship and, as the years go on and on, one of two possibilities ensues. Either one or both become openly and consciously dissatisfied. The soul needs to surge ahead, to find and to be found so as to dissolve separateness regardless of how much the other side of the personality fears it and is tempted by inertia. This dissatisfaction is either conscious—although in most instances one is unaware of the real reason for it—or unconscious; in either case the dissatisfaction is stronger than the temptation of the comfort of inertia and sluggishness. Then the marriage will be disrupted and one or both partners delude themselves into thinking that it will be different with a new partner, particularly after eros has perhaps struck again. As long as this principle is not understood, a person may go from one partnership to another, sustaining his feelings only as long as eros is at work.

The second possibility is that the temptation of "peace" is stronger. Then the partners remain together and they may certainly fulfill something together, but a great unfulfilled need will always lurk in their souls. Man is by nature the more active and adventurous; he tends to be as you call it, polygamous and therefore tempted much more to infidelity than woman. Thus you will also understand why man tends to be polygamous and what is the underlying motive for man's inclination to be unfaithful. Woman tends much more to be sluggish and is therefore better prepared to compromise. This is why she is monogamous. There are, of course, exceptions in both sexes.

Such infidelity is often equally puzzling to both partners, to the active one as much as to the "victim." They do not understand. The unfaithful one may suffer just as much as the one to whom he is unfaithful. In this possibility, that of compromise, both stagnate, at least in one very important aspect of their soul development. They find refuge in the steady comfort of their relationship. They may even believe that they are happy in it, and this may be true to some degree. The advantages of friendship, companionship, mutual respect and a pleasant life together with a pleasantly established routine outweigh the unrest of the soul and they may have enough discipline to remain faithful to one another. Yet an important element of their relationship is missing: the revealing of soul to soul as much as possible.

Only when two people do this can they be purified together and thus help each other, even without actually doing the work that this path entails. It could be thinkable that two developed souls who have this knowledge of purification in their subconscious, though ignoring the various steps of these teachings, can yet fulfill one another by revealing themselves, by searching the depths of the other's soul. Thus what is in the soul emerges into their conscious minds and purification takes place. Simultaneously, the life spark is maintained in the relationship so that it can never stagnate into a "dead end."

For you who are on this path, how much easier it will be to avoid the pitfalls and dangers of marital relationship and to repair damage that has occurred unwittingly. Should you find yourself alone, you may, by this knowledge and this truth, repair the damage that you have done to your own soul through the wrong concepts that slumber in you. You may discover your fear of the great adventurous journey with another, which is the explanation of why you are alone. This understanding will make it easier and may even enable your emotions to change sufficiently so that your outer life may change too. This depends on you. He who is unwilling to take the risk of this great adventure upon himself cannot succeed in the greatest venture humanity knows—marriage.

In this way, my dear friends, you not only maintain eros, that vibrating life-force, but you also transform it into true love. Only in this true partnership of love and eros can you discover in your partner new levels of being that you have heretofore not perceived. And you yourself will be purified by putting away your pride and revealing yourself as you really are. In this way, your relationship will always be new, regardless of how well you think you know each other already. All masks must fall, not only the superficial ones but the real ones, those you may not even be aware of. Then your love will remain alive. It will never be static, it will never stagnate. You will never have to search elsewhere. There is so much to see and discover in this land of the other soul you have chosen, whom you continue to respect but in whom you seem to miss the life-spark that once brought you together. You will never have to be afraid of losing the love of your beloved; this fear will have justification only if you refrain from risking the journey together.

This, my friends, is marriage in its true sense and the only way it can be the glory it is supposed to be. Each of you should think deeply about whether you are afraid to leave the four walls of your own separateness. Some of my friends are unaware that to stay separate is almost a conscious wish. With many of you it is this way: you desire marriage because one part of you yearns for it—and also because you do not want to be alone. Quite superficial and vain reasons may be added to explain the deep yearning within your soul. But aside from this yearning and aside from the superficial selfish motives of your unfulfilled desire for partnership, there must also be an unwillingness to really share your life in its deepest sense, and unwillingness to risk the journey and adventure of revealing yourself. An integral part of the life experience remains to be fulfilled by you, if not in this life, then in future ones.

Only when you meet love, life and the other being in such readiness, will you be able to bestow the greatest gift on your beloved, namely yourself, your real self. And then you must inevitably receive the same gift from your beloved. But to do that, a certain emotional and spiritual maturity has to exist. If this maturity is present, you will intuitively choose the right partner, one who has, in essence, the same maturity and readiness to embark on this journey. The choice of a partner who is unwilling to do so comes out of the hidden fear of undertaking it yourself. You magnetically draw people and situations toward you that correspond to your subconscious desires and fears. You know that.

Humanity, on the whole, is very far from this ideal, but that does not change the idea or the ideal. In the meantime, you have to learn to make the best of it. And you who are fortunate enough to be on this path can learn much wherever you stand, be it only in understanding why you cannot realize the happiness that your soul yearns for. To discover this is already a great deal and will enable you to get nearer to the realization—in this life or in future ones. Whatever your situation is, whether you have a partner or whether you are alone, search your heart and it will furnish the answer to your conflict. The answer must come from within yourself and, in all probability, it will be in connection with your own unwillingness, your fear and ignorance of these facts. Search and you will know. Understand what God's purpose is in the partnership of love: the complete mutual relation of one soul to another—not a superficial revelation.

Physical revelation is easy for many, and emotionally you go up to a certain degree—usually as far as eros carries you. But then you lock the door and that is the moment when your trouble begins. There are many who are not willing to reveal anything. They want to remain alone and aloof. They will not touch the experience of revealing themselves, and of finding the soul of the other person. They avoid this in every way they can.

My dear ones, now you will understand how important the erotic principle is in your sphere. It helps many who may be unwilling and unprepared for the love experience. It is what you call "falling in love" or "romance." In this way the personality gets a taste of what the ideal love could be. As I said before, many use this feeling of happiness carelessly and greedily, never passing the threshold into true love. True love demands much more from a person in a spiritual sense. If they do not meet this demand, they forfeit the goal for which the soul strives. This extreme is as wrong as the other wherein a person locks the doors so tightly that even the potent force of eros cannot enter. But unless the door is too tightly bolted, it does come to you at certain stages of life. Whether you can then bridge eros into love depends on you, your development, your willingness, your courage, your humility to reveal yourself.

Are there any questions in connection with this subject, my dear friends?

QUESTION: It is so difficult for a woman to talk to a man. Men don't answer when one tries to get into a conversation touching emotional understanding. That makes it very, very difficult for the woman.

ANSWER: Here is a great error, my dear. But let us first establish one fact that should be well understood. Woman is by nature more emotionally inclined. Man by nature is more spiritually, or on a lower level, intellectually inclined. By that I do not mean that he has to be "an intellectual." It is simply that usually the reasoning faculty is stronger in man. The revealing of his emotions is a very difficult step for a man. In this a woman can help him. The man will help the woman in other ways. The mistake you make is in thinking that revelation and the meeting of souls is brought about by talking. Oh, it may be a temporary crutch, it may be one detail; or rather, it may simply be a tool, a means of expressing certain facets. But this is all. It is not in the talking that you find the other soul or that you reveal yourself. As I have said, this may be a part of it. It is in the being that this whole and basic attitude is determined.

It is the woman who is the stronger emotionally. For her it is usually easier to muster the courage to meet soul to soul and touch the deepest core of longing that is also in man. If she can use her intuition and reach that part of her partner, he will respond provided he has the maturity. He must respond. Whether or not this response comes occasionally in the course of a conversation is not so important. It is not in question whether a verbal discussion serves in reaching the other soul. Certainly, speaking is a part of it, together with all the other faculties. But the ability to speak about things is not the determining factor. First the inner basis has to be established. Then you will be flexible enough to use all the faculties God has given you. Finding and meeting the other soul goes into the state of inner being; the doing is only an incidental result, a mere detail which is part of the outer manifestation. Is that clear?

QUESTION: Yes, it is clear. And I think it is wonderful. In other words, it is the task of the woman to find the other soul.

ANSWER: It may often be that it is easier for the woman to take the first necessary steps after eros is no longer working on its own momentum. But both have to have the basic willingness to go on the journey together. As stated before, the woman often finds it easier to reveal herself, to let the emotions come out. The mature woman who is earnestly willing to undertake the adventure of true marriage will have the mature and healthy instinct to find the right partner. The same applies to the man, of course.

Once this principle of willingness exists in both, either one may lead the way. It does not make any difference who starts. It may often be the woman, but it may also be the man at times. Whoever starts it, a time will come when the other one will also lead and help. In a relationship that is alive, healthy and flexible it must alternate and change constantly. And at any given time, whoever is the stronger, the leader, will help in the liberation of the other. For this is liberation—liberating the other soul from the prison of loneliness and liberating the self. This prison may even appear comfortable if you live and stagnate in it long enough. One should not wait for the other to start. He who is at that instant more mature and courageous will start, and will thereby raise the maturity of the other which in turn may then surpass his own. Thus, the helper becomes the helped; the liberator becomes the liberated.

QUESTION: When you talk about the revelation of one soul to another, does this mean that, on a higher level, this is the way the soul reveals itself to God?

ANSWER: It is the same thing. But before you can truly reveal yourself to God, you have to learn to reveal yourself to another beloved human being. And when you do that, you reveal yourself to God too. Many people want to start with revealing themselves to God directly, to the personal God. By actually, deep in their hearts, such revelation to God is only a subterfuge because it is so abstract and remote. What they reveal no other human being can see or hear. One is still alone. One does not have to do the one thing that seems so risky and that requires so much humility and thus appears humiliating. By revealing yourself to another human being, you accomplish so much that cannot be accomplished by revelation to God who knows you anyway, and who really does not need your revelation.

When you find the other soul and meet it, you fulfill your destiny. When you find another soul, you also find another particle of God, and if you reveal your own soul, you reveal a particle of God and give something divine to another person.

When eros comes to you, it will lift you up far enough so that you will sense and know what it is in you that longs for this experience and what is your true self, which is longing to reveal itself. Without eros, you are merely aware of the outer lazy layers.

Do not avoid eros when it wants to come to you. If you understand the spiritual idea behind it, you will use it wisely. God will then be able to lead you properly and enable you to make the best of it—the helping of another being and yourself into true love, where purification must be an integral part. Although it manifests differently than in your work on the path, the work will help you towards the same type of purification.

QUESTION: Is it possible for a soul to be so rich that he can reveal himself to more than one soul?

ANSWER: My dear friend, do you ask that facetiously?

QUESTION: No, I do not. I am asking whether polygamy is within the scheme of spiritual law.

ANSWER: No, it certainly is not. And when someone thinks it may be within the scheme of spiritual development, it is a subterfuge. The personality is looking for the right partner. Either he is too immature to have found the right partner, or the right partner is there and the polygamous person is simply carried away by eros' momentum, never lifting this force up into the volitional love that demands overcoming and working in order to pass the threshold I mentioned before.

In cases like this, the adventurous personality is looking and looking, always finding another part of a being, always revealing himself only so far and no further. Or perhaps each time he reveals another facet of his personality, but when it comes to the inner nucleus of the personality, the door is shut, eros departs and a new search is started. Each time, it is a disappointment that can only be understood when you understand these truths.

Raw sexual instinct also enters into the longing for this great journey, but sexual satisfaction begins to suffer if the relationship is not kept on the level I show you here. It is, in fact, inevitably of short duration. It is not a question of richness in revealing oneself to many. In such cases one either reveals the same wares all over again to new partners, or, as said before, he displays different facets. The more partners you try to share yourself with, the less you give to each. That is inevitably so. It cannot be different.

QUESTION: Certain people believe that they can cut out sex and eros, that they can cut out the desire for a partner and live completely for love of humanity. Do you think it is possible that man or woman can swear off this part of life?

ANSWER: It is possible, but it is certainly not healthy or honest. I might say that there is perhaps one person in ten million who may have such a task. That may be possible. It may be a particular karma or fate, either because that soul is already so developed, has gone through the true partnership experience and comes for a specific mission, or because of certain karmic debts that have to be paid off. But in most cases—and here I can safely generalize—if it happens, it is unhealthy, it is an escape and the real reason is fear of love, fear of the life experience, all of which is rationalized into sacrifice. To anyone who would come to me with just such a problem, I would say, "Examine yourself, go below the surface layers of your conscious reasoning and explanations for your attitude in this respect. Try to find out whether you fear love and disappointment. Isn't it more comfortable to just live for yourself and have no difficulties? Isn't that what you feel deep inside and which you want to cover up with other reasons?

This great humanitarian work you want to do may be a worthy cause, indeed, but do you really think one excludes the other?

Wouldn't it be much more likely that the great task you have taken upon yourself would be better fulfilled if you learned personal love too?"

If all these questions are truthfully answered, such a person would be bound to see that he is escaping. Personal love and fulfillment is man's and woman's destiny in most cases, for so much can be learned through it that cannot be learned in any other way. And to make a durable and solid relationship in a marriage is the greatest victory man can achieve, for it is one of the most difficult things there is, as you can well see in your world. This life-experience will bring the soul closer to God than the lukewarm good deed.

QUESTION: I was going to ask in connection with my previous question: celibacy is supposed to be a highly spiritualized form of development in certain religious sects. On the other hand there is polygamy which also is recognized in religion—the Mormons, for instance. I understand what you said. But how do you justify these attitudes on the part of people who are supposed to look for unity with God?

ANSWER: Human error exists in every religion. In one religion it may be one error, in another religion a different one. Here you simply have two extremes. When such dogmas or rules come into existence in the various religions, whether at one extreme or another, it is always a rationalization and subterfuge to which the individual soul constantly resorts. This is an attempt to explain away the counter currents of the fearful or greedy soul with good motives.

There is another thing I ought to mention regarding the common belief that anything pertaining to sex is sinful. The sex instinct arises in the infant. The more immature the creature, the more is sex separated from love, and therefore the more selfish it is. Anything without love is "sinful," if you want to use this word. Nothing that is coupled with love is wrong—or sinful.

There is no such thing as a force, a principle or an idea that can be regarded as sinful, as such—not sex or anything else.

Thus, in the growing child who is naturally immature, the sex drive will first manifest selfishly. Only if and when the whole personality grows and matures harmoniously will sex become incorporated with love. But due to the fact that, out of ignorance, humanity has long believed that sex as such is sinful, it was kept hidden and, therefore, this part of the personality could not possibly grow up. Nothing that remains in hiding can grow; you know that. Therefore, even in many grown-ups, sex remains childish and separate from love. And this, in turn, led mankind to believe more and more that sex is a sin and that the truly spiritual person must abstain from it. Thus one of those oft mentioned vicious circles came into existence.

Because of this belief, the sex instinct could not grow and melt in with the love-force. Consequently, sex is, in fact, often selfish and loveless, raw and animalistic. If people who realize—and they are beginning to do so more and more—that the sex instinct is as natural and God-given as any other universal force and in itself not more sinful than other existing forces, they would then break this vicious circle and more human beings would let their sex drives mature and mingle with love—and with eros, for that matter.

How many people exist for whom sex is completely separate from love! They not only suffer from a bad conscience when the sex urge manifests, but they also find themselves in a position of being unable to handle sexual feelings with the person they really love. This exists quite often in some measure, although it does seem extreme. Because of these conditions and this vicious circle, humanity came to believe that you cannot find God when you respond to your sex urges. This is all wrong; you cannot kill off something that is alive. You can only hide it so that it will come out in other ways that may be much more harmful. Only in the very rarest of cases does the sex force really become sublimated so as to make this creative force manifest in other realms. "Sublimation" in its real sense can never occur when there is fear and escape involved, as is the case with most human beings.

QUESTION: If two young people fall in love and marry and they are not well matched and they don't understand each other, is it possible that these two people could go on this journey together and have a good marriage?

ANSWER: If both are willing to learn to love one another and gain maturity together. Even where an immature choice was made, it could still become a successful marriage, but only if both are willing and are clearly aware of what marriage is supposed to be. If both lack the will and sense of responsibility for that, they will not have the desire to make such a journey together.

QUESTION: Where does the love and understanding of friendship fit into this picture? Just friendship between two people?

ANSWER: Friendship is brotherly love. That friendship can also exist between man and woman, but this is something else again. Eros may want to sneak in, so to speak, but still, will and reason can direct the way in which feelings take their course. That is why in the well-balanced personality, reason must play a role and will help to direct the emotions, preventing the feelings from going into an improper channel. There, discretion and the balance between reason, emotion, and will is necessary.

QUESTION: Is divorce against spiritual law?

ANSWER: Not necessarily. We do not have fixed rules such as that. There are, of course, cases when divorce is an easy way out, a mere escape. There are other cases when divorce is reasonable because the choice was made in immaturity and both lack the desire to fulfill the responsibility of marriage in its true sense. If only one is willing—or neither—divorce is better than staying together and making a farce out of marriage. Unless both are willing to take this journey together, it is better to break clean than to let one prevent the growth of the other. That happens. It is better to terminate a mistake than to remain indefinitely in it without finding an effective remedy.

One should not, however, go out of marriage lightly. Even though it was a mistake and does not work, one should try to find the reasons and do one's very best to search out and perhaps get over the hurdles that are in the way due to one's own inner mistakes and try to make the best of it, if both are in any way willing. One can learn a lot from one's past and present mistakes. It cannot be generalized that divorce is either wrong in any case or that it is always right. One should certainly do one's best, even if the marriage is not the ideal experience that I discussed tonight. Few people are ready and mature enough for it. You can make yourself ready by trying to make the best of your past mistakes and learn from them.

My dearest friends, think very well about what I have said. There is much food for thought in what I told you, for each of you here, for all those who are not here but will read my words. There is not a single friend who cannot learn something.

I want to close this evening with the assurance to all of you that we, in the spirit world, are deeply grateful to God for your good efforts, for your improvement. It is our greatest joy and our greatest happiness. And so, my dear ones, receive the blessings of the Lord again; may your hearts be filled by this wonderful strength coming to you from the world of light and truth. Go in peace and in happiness, my dear ones, each one of you. Be in God!

Emotional Growth and Its Function

G R E E T I N G S, my dearest friends. God bless each one of you; blessed is this hour.

In order to know yourself on a deeper level, it becomes increasingly necessary to allow all emotions to reach surface awareness, so as to understand these emotions and to allow them to mature. This has been discussed before and your individual work points more and more in that direction. Most of you also know the great resistance you have to overcome. Some of you have tasted the difficulties you have to face in order to overcome this resistance. You all stand more or less at different vantage points in this respect. Some of you recognize your own resistance for what it is and consciously battle against it. You recognize the signs. You recognize the evasion and escape-mechanism at work. But some of you are still so involved in the resistance itself that you are unaware of the obstructions you put in your way. Hence it is necessary that I discuss the mechanism of this resistance.

In order to understand it, let us first be clear about the unity of the human personality. A human being who functions harmoniously has developed the physical, the mental, and the emotional side of his nature. These three spheres are supposed to function harmoniously, each helping the other rather than one faculty being used to subdue another as so often is the case. If one function is underdeveloped, disharmony in the entire human structure results and also a crippling of the entire personality.

This much you know from our previous talks and your own previous findings. Now let us further understand what causes man to particularly neglect, repress, and cripple the growth of his emotional nature. This is universal. Most human beings look after the physical self. They do more or less what is necessary to make it grow and remain healthy. And a good portion of mankind—comparatively speaking—cultivates the mental side. In order to do so, you learn, you use your brain, you use your thinking capacity, you absorb, you train your memory, you train your faculty of logical deduction, and all this furthers mental growth.

But why then is there a general neglect of man's emotional nature? There are good reasons for that, my friends. In order to gain more clarity about this subject, let us first understand the function of the emotional nature in man. It includes, first of all, the capacity to feel. The capacity to experience feeling is synonymous with the capacity to give and receive happiness. To the degree you shy away from any kind of emotional experience, to that extent also do you close the door to the experience of happiness. Moreover, the emotional side of your nature, when functioning, contains creative ability. To the degree that you close yourself off from emotional experience, to that very degree is the full potential of your creative ability hindered in manifesting itself. Contrary to what many of you may believe, the unfolding of creative ability is not a mere mental process. In fact, the intellect has much less to do with it than may appear at first glance, in spite of the fact that technical skill also becomes a necessity in order to represent the creative outflow and to give it full justice. Creative unfoldment is an intuitive process. And needless to say, intuition can function only to the degree that your emotional life is strong, healthy, and mature.

Therefore, the intuitive powers will be hindered to the degree that you have neglected emotional growth and to the degree that you have discouraged yourself from experiencing the world of feeling. Why is there such a predominant emphasis in your world today on physical and mental growth and a predominant neglect of emotional growth? Several general explanations could be advanced, but I would like to go immediately to the root of the problem bypassing the outer, general causes which are only symptoms of the root anyway.

In the world of feeling you experience the good and the bad, the happy and the unhappy, pleasure and pain. Contrary to registering these impressions mentally, such emotional experience really touches you. Since man's struggle is primarily for happiness, and since immature emotions lead to unhappiness, his secondary aim becomes the avoidance of unhappiness.

This creates the early, mostly unconscious conclusion: "If I do not feel, then I will not be unhappy." In other words, instead of taking the courageous and adequate step to live through negative, immature emotions in order to afford them the opportunity to grow and thus to become mature and constructive, the childish emotions are suppressed, put out of awareness, and buried so that they remain inadequate and destructive, even though the person is unaware of their existence.

Unhappy circumstances exist in every child's life; pain and disappointment exist. The less such pain and disappointment is a conscious experience and the more it lies in a vague, dull climate that you cannot even put your finger on and is just something to be taken for granted, the greater is the danger that unconsciously the resolution will be made, "I must not allow myself to feel if I wish to prevent the pain and the experience of unhappiness."

In the past we have discussed why this is a wrong conclusion and solution. But may I briefly recapitulate? Although it may be true that you dull your capacity for emotional experience, like an anesthesia, and therefore cannot feel immediate pain right now, it is also true that you dull your capacity for happiness and pleasure while not really avoiding the dreaded unhappiness in the long run. That is, the unhappiness you seem to avoid comes to you in a different and much more painful but indirect way. The bitter hurt of isolation, of loneliness, the gnawing feeling of having passed by life without experiencing its heights and its depths, without developing yourself to the most and best you can be, is the result of such cowardly evasion, such a wrong solution.

By such evasion, you do not experience life at its fullest. By withdrawing from pain, you withdraw from happiness and, most of all, you withdraw from experience. At one time or another—you may never remember the conscious intent—your solution was to dull the capacity to feel in order to avoid pain. And from that moment onward, you withdrew from living, loving, experiencing—from everything that makes life rich and rewarding. In addition, the result is that your intuitive powers are dulled as well as your creative faculties. You only function to a tiny degree of your potential. The damage you have inflicted upon yourself with this solution, and go on inflicting upon yourself as long you adhere to this pseudo-solution, eludes your comprehension and evaluation at the present time.

Since this was your defense mechanism against unhappiness to begin with, it is understandable that unconsciously you fight tooth and nail against giving up what seems to you a vital protection. You do not realize that not only do you miss out on life's richness, life's rewards, your own full potential, but you do not really avoid unhappiness, as already indicated. This painful isolation was not willingly chosen by you and therefore is not accepted as a price to be paid. Rather, it came as a necessary byproduct of your pseudo-solution, and with this defense mechanism at work, the child in you hopes for and fights to receive what you cannot possibly receive. In other words, somewhere deep inside, you hope and believe that it is possible to belong and to be loved while you dull your world of feeling into a state of numbness and thereby prohibit yourself from truly loving others. Yes, you may need others and this need may appear as love to you, but now you know that this is not the same. Inside, you hope and believe it possible to unite with others, to communicate in a rewarding and satisfying way with the world around you, while you put up a wall of pseudo-protection against the impact of emotional experience. If and when you cannot help but feel, you are busy hiding such feelings from yourself and others. How can you receive what you yearn for—love, belonging, communication—if you neither feel nor express the occasional glimpses of feelings that the still healthy part in you strives for? You cannot have it both ways, though the child in you never wants to accept that.

Since you "protect" yourself in this foolish manner, you isolate yourself, thus exposing yourself much more to that which you strive to avoid. Hence you miss out doubly: you do not avoid that which you fear—not really and not in the long run—and you miss out on all you could have if you did not run away from living. For living and feeling are one. The lack of love and fulfillment you must increasingly crave makes you blame others, circumstances, the fates, or bad luck, instead of seeing how you are responsible for it. You resist such insight because you sense that the moment you see it fully, you will have to change and you can no longer cling to the comfortable but unrealizable hope that you can have what you want without meeting the necessary conditions to get it. If you want happiness you must be willing to give it. How can you give it if you are unwilling and unable to feel as much as you are capable of feeling? Realize that it is you who caused this state of unfulfillment, and it is you who can still change it, regardless of your physical age.

Another reason for resorting to this unsuccessful pseudo-solution is the following: as in everything else, feeling and emotional expression can be mature and constructive or immature and destructive. As a child you possessed an immature body and mind and therefore, quite naturally, an immature emotional structure. Most of you gave your body and mind a chance to grow out of immaturity and to reach a certain physical and mental maturity. Let me give you an example on the physical level: an infant will feel the strong urge to use its vocal cords. This is an instinct with the function of promoting the growth of certain organic matter through strong use of the vocal cords. When the baby is screaming, it is not pleasant but it is a period of transition that leads to strong healthy organs in this particular respect. Not going through this unpleasant time, suppressing the instinctual urge to scream, would eventually damage and weaken the respective organs. The urge to indulge in strong physical exercise has the same function, or the urge, at times, to eat perhaps more than necessary. All this is part of the growing process. To stop this growing process with the excuse that there is the danger of over-exertion and over-eating would be foolish and damaging. I do not mean a reasonable halt to something that is obviously harmful; I mean ceasing to use the muscles at all, to feed the child at all, with the rationalization that such exercise and food, per se, might lead to painful experiences.

Yet this is done with your emotional self. You stop its functioning because you consider the growing, transitional period so dangerous that you proceed to stop growth altogether. You not only hinder excesses as a result of this reasoning, but you also hinder all the transitory functioning which alone can lead to constructive mature emotions. Since this is more or less the case with every one of you, the period has to be gone through now. It just cannot be skipped altogether; if you do, your overall development will be lopsided and, therefore, your personality structure crippled.

When your mental processes mature, you have to go through transitional periods too. You not only learn, you are also bound to make mistakes. In your younger years you often hold opinions which, later, you grow out of. While later you see that these opinions are not as "right" as they seemed to you during your youth and see another side that earlier you neglected to see, it was nevertheless beneficial for you to go through these times of error. How could you appreciate truth if you had not gone through error? You can never gain truth by avoiding error. It strengthens your mental faculties, your logic, your power of deduction and your range. Without being allowed to make mistakes in your thinking, in your opinions, your mental faculties could not grow.

Strangely enough, there is much less resistance in human nature to the necessary growing pains of the physical and mental sides of the personality, than there is to the growth of the emotional nature. It is entirely overlooked that emotional growing pains are necessary too, and that they are constructive and beneficial. Without consciously thinking about it in these terms, you believe that the emotional growth-process should come about without growing pains. Most of the time, it is altogether overlooked that this area exists at all, let alone that it needs growth; neither do you know how such growth is to be accomplished. You, who are on this path ought to begin to understand this. If you do, your resistance and insistence on remaining stale in this respect, on remaining deadened and dulled will finally give way and you will no longer object to going through a period of growth now.

In this growing period, immature emotions have to express themselves. Only as they are allowed expression, so that you can understand their meaning and significance, will you finally reach a point when you no longer need such immature emotions. This will not happen through a process of will, an outer mental decision which represses what is still a part of your emotional being, but through an organic process of emotional growth wherein feelings will naturally change their direction, their aim, their intensity, their nature. But this can only be done if you experience your emotions as they exist in you now.

When you were hurt as a child, your reactions were anger, resentment, hate—sometimes to a very strong degree. If you prevent yourself from consciously experiencing these emotions, you will not get rid of them; you will not enable healthy mature emotions to follow in their place, you will simply repress existing feelings. You bury them and deceive yourself that you do not feel what you actually still feel. Since you dull your capacity to feel, you become unaware of what exists underneath. Then you superimpose feelings that you think you ought to have but which you do not really and truly have.

You all operate—some more, some less—with feelings that are not genuinely yours, with feelings you think you ought to have but do not have. Underneath, something entirely different is taking place. Only in times of extreme crisis do these actual feelings reach the surface. Then you believe it is the crisis that has caused these reactions in you. You wish to ignore the fact that the crisis only made it impossible for you to deceive yourself, that crisis reactivated the still immature emotions. That the crisis itself is the effect of hidden emotional immaturity, as well as of existing self-deception, just does not penetrate your mind.

The fact that you put raw, destructive, immature emotions out of sight instead of growing out of them and then deceive yourself, believing you are a much more integrated and mature person that you actually are, is not only dishonesty, hypocrisy, and self-deception, but it also leads you more deeply into isolation, unhappiness, alienation from yourself, and unsuccessful, unrewarding patterns that you repeat over and over again. The result of all this seems to confirm your pseudo-solution, your defense-mechanism, but this is a very misleading conclusion.

Immature emotions earned you punishment as a child; either they caused you pain in actuality, or expressing them produced an undesired result. Either you lost something you wanted, such as the affection of certain people for instance, or a desired goal was made impossible when you expressed what you really felt—which then became an additional reason why you hindered self-expression. Consequently, as you perceived such emotions to be undesirable, you proceeded to whisk them also out of your own sight. This shows that you found it necessary to do so because you did not want to be hurt, you did not wish to experience the pain of feeling unhappiness. You also found it necessary to repress existing emotions because the expression of the negative resulted in an undesirable end.

You might say that because the latter is true, your procedure is therefore valid, necessary and self-preserving. You will rightly say that if you live out your negative emotions, the world will punish you in one form or another. Yes, my friends, this is true. Immature emotions are indeed destructive and will indeed bring you disadvantages. But your error lies in the thought—conscious or unconscious—that to be aware of what you feel and to give vent to it in action are one and the same. You cannot discriminate between the two courses of action. Neither can you discriminate between a constructive aim for which it is necessary to express and talk about what you feel, at the right place, with the right people; and the destructiveness of heedlessly letting go all control, of not choosing the right aim, the right place, and the right people, of not wanting to use such expression as would gain you insight into yourself. If you merely let go out of a lack of discipline, without an aim, and then expose negative emotions, it is indeed destructive.

Try to distinguish between constructive and destructive aims, try to realize the purpose and then develop the courage and humility to allow yourself to be aware of what you really feel and to express it when it is meaningful. If you do this, then you will see the tremendous difference between merely allowing immature and destructive emotions to come to the fore in order to relieve yourself of pressure and give them an outlet without aim or meaning and the purposeful activity of re-experiencing all the feelings that once existed in you and that still exist in you—even if you are convinced that this is no longer the case. What has not been properly assimilated in emotional experience but has instead been repressed will constantly be reactivated by present situations that remind you in one way or another of the original situation. Such a "reminder" may not be factual. It can be an emotional climate, a symbolic association that lodges exclusively in the subconscious. But as you learn to become aware of what is really going on in you, you will also become aware of such "reminders." You will also become aware that often you actually feel very much the opposite of what you force yourself to feel.

As the first few tentative steps are taken in the direction of becoming aware of what you feel and expressing it in a direct way, without finding reasons and excuses, without rationalizing it, you will gain an understanding about yourself such as you never had before. You will actively feel the growing process at work, because you actively participate with your innermost self, not merely with outer gestures. You will not only begin to understand what brought on many undesired results, but how it is in your power to change them. You will also understand the interaction between yourself and others: how your unconscious distorted pattern has affected others in exactly the opposite of the way you originally wanted. This will give you an inner understanding about the process of communication.

This is the only way emotions can mature. By going through the period that was missed in childhood and adolescence, the emotions will finally mature and you will no longer need to fear the power of those emotions which you cannot control when you merely put them out of awareness. You will be able to trust them, to be guided by them—for that is the final aim of the mature and well-functioning person. I might say that, to some degree, this has happened to all of you. There are times when you allow yourself to be guided by your power of intuition. But it happens more as an exception than as a rule. It cannot happen as a rule as long as your emotions remain destructive and childish; they are unreliable in this state. Since you discourage their growth, you live by your mental faculties only—and they are secondary in efficiency. When healthy emotions make your intuition reliable, there will be a mutual harmony between the mental and emotional faculties. One will not contradict the other. As long as you cannot rely on your intuitive processes, you must be insecure and lacking in self-confidence. You try to make up for this by relying on others, on false religion. This makes you weak and helpless. But if you have mature, strong emotions, you will trust yourself and therein find a security you never dreamed existed.

After the first painful release of negative emotions, you will find a certain relief in the realization that poisonous matter has left your system in a manner that was not destructive for you or for others. After thus having gained insight and understanding, new, warm, good emotions will come out of you that could not express themselves so long as the negative emotions were held in check. You will also learn to discriminate between genuine good feelings and the false good feelings that you superimpose out of the need to maintain your idealized self-image: "This is the way I should be." Because you cling to this idealized self-image, you cannot find your real self. Because this is so, you do not have the courage to accept the fact that a comparatively large area of your personality is still childish, incomplete, and imperfect. It falls considerably short of what you want to appear to be.

You hold on to the illusion of yourself, in the wrong belief that if you acknowledge the fallacy, you will be destroyed. You never realize that this is the first necessary step to destroy your destructive processes and to build a real solid self that will stand on firm ground. For only in the mature emotions, in the courage to make this maturity and growth possible, will you gain the security within yourself you so ardently hunt for elsewhere. You constantly reach for false solutions in order to create an illusion of security that can be pulled from under your feet at the slightest provocation because it is unreal.

So, build your security. You have nothing to fear in becoming aware of what is already in you. Looking away from what is does not cause it to cease to exist. Therefore, it is wise on your part to want to look at, to face and to acknowledge that which is in you—no more and no less! To believe that it harms you more to know what you feel and are than not to know, is extremely foolish. Yet to some degree, that is exactly what you all do. That is the nature of your resistance to accepting and facing yourself. Only after you face what is in you will your much more mature intellect be able to make the decision as to whether these inner behavior patterns are worth keeping or not. You are not forced to give up what seems a protection to you. But look at it with the clear and lucid eyes of truth. That is all I ask you to do. You have nothing to fear from it.

After you have evaluated the childish emotions, you will hold in your hand the key to growing up and becoming a wholly integrated and healthy human being. You will soon discover the fallacy that there is a danger in becoming aware of and expressing childish emotions. There is danger only if you let them go without control, without the discipline of expressing them with the specific aim of gaining a meaningful experience from it. It is not enough to say that there is no danger in such a constructive activity: it is the only way to alleviate the danger of your insecurity and of your pretense which you sense all the time and which makes you even more insecure and fearful of exposure. Deep inside you know of your pretense, of your false maturity, of your idealized self-image. And you shake because you know it and you think you defend it by continuing to close your eyes to it. You think you can whisk away the falsity by not acknowledging it. Actually, the truth is that you can grow out of the falsity only by first of all accepting its existence at the present time; owning up to it. Then and then only can you build a genuine self you can trust and rely on. Then you do not have to fear exposure.

And now, my friends, let us consider this subject in the light of spirituality. You all have come with the original idea of growing spiritually. And I might say that more or less all of you hope to accomplish this without tending to your emotional growth. You want to believe that the one is possible without the other. Needless to say, this a complete impossibility. In the course of this work and of the considerable success you have accomplished in the hard work of self-facing, sooner or later all of you will reach the point where you have to make up your mind as to whether you really want emotional growth or you still want to cling to the childish hope that spiritual growth is possible while you neglect the world of feeling and allow it to lie dormant without giving it the opportunity to grow. Let us examine this for a moment, my friends.

You all know, regardless of what religion or spiritual philosophy or teaching you follow, that love is the first and the greatest power. In the last analysis, it is the only power. Most of you have used this saying many times. But I wonder, my friends, whether you have realized that all along you have spoken words, just words, never knowing that you have used empty words, while all the time you veered away from feeling, from experiencing, from the world of emotional reaction and experience! Now, how can you love if you do not let yourself feel? How can you love and at the same time remain what you choose to call "detached"? That means remaining personally un-involved, that you not risk pain, disappointment, personal involvement. Can you love in such a comfortable way? Is love an intellectual process? Is love a lukewarm matter of laws, words, letters, regulations, and rules you talk about? Or is love a feeling that comes from deep within the soul, a warmth of flowing impact that cannot leave you indifferent and untouched? Is it not foremost a feeling, and only after the feeling is fully experienced and expressed, will wisdom, and perhaps even intellectual insight—as a by-product, so to speak—result from it?

How can you hope to gain spirituality—and spirituality, religion, and love are one—by neglecting your emotional processes? Think about this, my friends. Begin to see how you all sit back, hoping for a comfortable spirituality that leaves out your personal involvement in the world of feel-ings. After you see this clearly, you will comprehend how preposterous this attitude is. Your conscious or unconscious rationalizations in still denying the awareness and expression of your emotions, even though they are at the moment still destructive to quite a degree, will take on a different light in your own eyes. You will look upon your resistance to doing what is so nec-essary with a little more understanding and truth. Any spiritual develop-ment is a farce if you deny this part of your being. If you do not have the courage to allow the negative in you to reach your surface awareness, how can healthy, strong emotions fill your being? If you cannot deal with the negative because it is out of your awareness, this very same negative element will stand in the way of the positive.

Those of you who now follow this path and do what is so necessary, will first experience a host of negative feelings. But after these are dealt with and properly understood, warm, mature, constructive feelings will evolve. You will feel warmth, compassion, good involvement such as you never thought possible. You will no longer feel yourself isolated. You will begin to truly relate to others in truth and reality, not in falsehood and self-deception. When this happens, a new security and respect for yourself will become part of you. You will begin to trust and like yourself.

QUESTION: I would like to ask, how about the prophets or other holy people? Were they grown emotionally? Wasn't it just love they gave?

ANSWER: Just love they gave? Could love be given without emotional maturity?

QUESTION: Is faith in God and love without emotional maturity possible?

ANSWER: That is impossible, if we speak about real love, the willingness to be personally involved, and not about the childish need to be loved and cherished which is so often confused with love. For real love and real, genuine faith to exist, emotional maturity is a necessary basis. Love and faith and emotional immaturity are mutually exclusive, my child. The ability to love is a direct outcome of emotional maturity and growth. True faith in God, in the sense of true religion as opposed to false religion, is again a matter of emotional maturity, because true religion is self-dependent. It does not cling to a father-authority out of the need to be protected. False faith and false love always have the strong emotional connotation of *need*. True love and true faith come out of strength, out of self-reliance, and self-responsibility. All these are attributes of emotional maturity. And only with strength, self-reliance and self-responsibility is true love, involvement, and faith possible. Anyone who ever attained spiritual growth, known or unknown in history, had to have emotional maturity.

QUESTION: If someone in this work finds wild emotions going back to childhood, how is it possible to handle this and substitute for them and let them disintegrate if one does not happen to have with him the other person who helps in this work? At the time, let us say twice a month, that we have the opportunity to express them, we may not feel such emotions while we strongly feel them at other times. If one is on one's own, what is the right way to handle it at the brink of the moment when these emotions come up?

ANSWER: In the first place, it is significant if emotions only come out when one is not actively doing this work with the so-called helper. This in itself points to a strong resistance. It is the long, drawn out result of consistent repression. Due to such repression, the emotions that come out first will appear at inopportune moments and will be so strong as to confuse the person. But after a comparatively short time, with the inner will truly determined to face the self in its entirety, destructive emotions will not only appear at the proper time and in the proper place, but you will be able to handle them with a meaningful result. This state points to resistance, repression, and the fact that inward struggle and hate still exist with the childish wish that manifest conflicts should be resolved while the basic defense-mechanism is left untouched. If destructive emotions govern you, instead of your being able to govern them without repression, it is a form of temper-tantrum in which the psyche says, "You see, you have forced me to do this, and now see where this leads to." If such subtle hidden emotions can be detected, it will alleviate any danger of negative emotions taking on a power that the personality cannot handle.

In the second place, it is important that you do not feel guilty about the existence of such emotions, which are probably incompatible with the image you have of yourself. If you learn to accept the reality of yourself instead of your mistaken self-image, the strength of negative emotions will abate. Yes you will, of course, experience negative emotions, but you will never fear that they can lead you toward a lack of self-control. Let me put it this way: the strong impact of negative emotions, to the point that you fear that you are unable to handle them, is due not so much to their existence per se, but due to the lack of acceptance on your part that you are not your idealized self. The negative emotions in themselves would be much less disturbing if you did not cling to the idealized self while struggling to give it up. Once you have accepted yourself as you now happen to be and have made the inner decision to part with the illusion of yourself, you will feel much more at ease. You will become capable of experiencing negative emotions in a meaningful way that is growth-producing. You will derive insight from them, even if you are alone at the moment. Moreover, emotions will come up during working sessions and will yield even greater insight if they are expressed and worked with.

So, I cannot give you rules to observe. I can only point to the reason behind this manifestation. If you truly absorb it, wish to understand it and go on from there, this will help you a great deal. Of course, this is addressed to all of my friends.

QUESTION: That means that the emotions as such are not dangerous, it is our disappointment in ourselves that makes them so powerful? Or dangerous?

ANSWER: Yes, that is right. But they need not be dangerous if you do not want them to be. If inner anger is not properly understood and released in a constructive way such as you learn on this path, the so-called temper tantrum takes place and the child in you lashes out, destroying others and the self. Find this lashing-out child, and you will be in control of evolving negative emotions without repressing them, but expressing them constructively and learning from them. Find the area in which you resent not being taken care of, not being given all you want. Once you are aware of the reason for all this anger, you will be able to humor yourself because you will see the preposterous demands of the child in you. This is the work you have to do in this particular phase. This is a crucial and decisive milestone on your road. When you get over this particular hump, the work will proceed much more easily. Again, I repeat, this is a general explanation for all who may find this answer useful. Whenever you are afraid of losing control, I advise you to think of the image you have of yourself; of what you think you should be, as opposed to the emotions that actually come to the fore. The moment you see this discrepancy, you will no longer feel threatened by the negative emotions. You will be able to handle them. This is the best advice for you in this respect. Find in yourself the element where you are angry at the world for not allowing you to be your idealized self-image; where you feel it prevents you from being what you could be without its interference. Once you are aware of such emotional reactions, you will again come a great step forward.

You see, my friends, your misunderstanding is that you think the harm comes from the existence of the negative emotions as such. It does not. It comes from your nonacceptance of your real self; from the blame you throw into the world for not allowing you to be what you feel you could be if the world would let you. This is the nature of such strong, powerful emotions, and they can endanger you only as long as you are unaware of their nature. Therefore, seek their meaning. Seek their true message and you will never have to fear.

QUESTION: How can you be sure that I mean it when I say I love a person? [a child asked this question]

ANSWER: My little son, I have this to say: the human being is not cut from one piece. There are very many contradictory emotions possible. You may love a particular person and then, perhaps in the next moment, you may feel hatred or resentment. The fact that you do, does not make it untrue that you also love that person. It is not true that if you occasionally feel hate, you never love and that you do not really feel love in other moments. Both are possible. You see, it is very important that a person understand why he occasionally feels hate, while he also loves. The reason for such occasional hate is always a hurt. If you are hurt, know it. Know why. It will not harm you, because the next step in your development will be that you realize that your own lack of understanding causes the hurt and therefore the hatred. Then the next step will be, as you grow still more mature, that you gain understanding and therefore you will no longer be hurt and will not hate.

If, for the moment, you merely understand that your hate does not annul your love, you will not feel guilty. You will know that you are hurt and why and therefore you will be able to say to yourself, "I love and I mean it, but I also hate because I feel hurt."

As you grow in the way of this path, little by little the negative emotions will disappear. But while they are still present, you must forgive yourself. You can easily do so when you realize that you still love, even while you hate and that you hate only because you are hurt. You need not expect of yourself that you always love and understand. No one can do that. But it can gradually come, very gradually. Hurt will grow less and therefore love will grow more.

You have a wonderful opportunity here, my friends, to make a side in you grow that has been neglected. This is true of some to a greater degree than others, but all of you have to persist in working on this particular phase. You have caused entirely unnecessary hindrances in your life. You have a wonderful opportunity to remedy this very unfortunate mistake that infects the entire human race.

With this, my dearest, dearest friends, I go from you. Blessings for each one of you. May you all gain further strength, further wisdom to conduct your life and your inner growth in such a way that you do not stand still. For this is the only thing that gives meaning to life—continuous growth. The better you accomplish this, the more will you be at peace with yourself. Blessings with all strength, love and warmth are given unto you. Be blessed, be in peace, be in God!

Connection Between the Ego and Universal Consciousness

REETINGS, my dearest friends. May this lecture give you renewed insight and strength so that your attempts to find yourself, to find your position, your situation in this life, where you belong, what you are, who you are, and how to fulfill yourself, become a little easier. May you find a new shaft of light through these words. It will be so if you truly open up to new aspects of perhaps the same ideas you have heard before but which as yet have not become a personally experienced truth for you.

The meaningfulness and fulfillment of one's life depend, in the last analysis, entirely on the relationship between man's ego and the universal life principle—the real self as we also call it. If this relationship is balanced, everything falls into place. All these lectures deal with this topic in one way or another and I always try to discuss it in different ways. This is necessary in order for you to finally experience the truth of these words.

Let us try to define again what the universal life principle is and how it manifests in man. The universal life principle is life itself. It is eternal consciousness in its deepest and highest sense. It is eternally moving and it is pleasure supreme. Since it is life, it cannot die. It is the essence of all that breathes, moves, vibrates. It knows all, for it is that which creates on and on, self-perpetuating because it cannot be untrue to its own nature.

Every individual consciousness is universal consciousness. It would not be correct to state that it is a part, for a part implies it is only a little of it, a fragment of a whole. Wherever consciousness exists at all, it is all of the original consciousness. This original consciousness, the creative life principle, individualizes itself in varied forms. When individualization passes a certain point and progresses beyond the state where it knows its connection with its origin, a disconnection comes into existence. Thus consciousness continues to exist and to contain the possibilities of universal consciousness, but it is oblivious of its own nature, its laws, and its potentials. This, in short, is the state of human consciousness as a whole.

When man begins to become aware of the life principle's ever-present nature, he discovers that it has always been there but that he has not noticed it because he was under the illusion of his separate existence. Therefore, it is not entirely accurate to state that "it manifests"; it would be correct to say "man begins to notice." He may notice its ever-present power as autonomous consciousness or as energy. The separated ego-personality possesses both, but the ego intelligence is by far inferior to the universal intelligence man potentially is, whether or not he realizes and utilizes it. The same applies to the energy. We will come back to this a little later.

These two aspects of universal life are not two separate factors, they are a oneness. Some people tend to be more open and receptive to one of these basic aspects as it is perceivable to man, while they are more prejudiced or ignorant in regard to the other one. With other people it may be just the opposite. Both must be experienced when the self realizes itself.

One of the universal life principle's basic characteristics—whether in its aspect of autonomous consciousness or as energy—is that it is spontaneous. It cannot manifest in any way other than spontaneously. It cannot possibly reveal itself as a result of a direct laborious process, arrived at in a cramped and over-concentrated state. Therefore its manifestation is always an indirect result. It occurs when it is least expected. By "indirect" I mean that man must, of course, make efforts. He must overcome resistance in order to face himself in truth, to admit his problems and shortcomings, to shed his illusions. This does require a great deal of effort. He must summon all the strength and courage he can possibly muster at all times. But the effort must be expended for the sake of seeing the truth about oneself, for the sake of giving up a specific illusion, for the sake of overcoming a barrier to wanting to be constructive rather than destructive, for the sake of seeing all there is to see in oneself—and not for the sake of an as yet theoretical process called self-realization that promises to feel good. If the latter is arduously forced and looked for, it cannot come. It comes as a by-product, as it were, although it is all that man can ever wish to attain.

Each step toward seeing the truth in the self, without any further subterfuge and self-deception, each step toward a genuine desire for constructive participation in the creative process of life, frees the self. Thus spontaneous processes begin to manifest. They are never volitional. Hence, the greater the fear of the unknown, the fear of letting go, the fear of unvolitional processes in one's own body-organization, the less is it possible to experience spontaneous manifestations of the life principle in the self. Such spontaneous manifestations may be inspirations of a hitherto unimaginable wisdom for solving one's personal problems or for cultivating one's creative talents. Or the life principle may manifest in a new way of experiencing and tasting life, giving a new flavor to all one is doing and seeing. It is as though an awareness had awakened within that thinks, feels, and experiences in an entirely new and vibrant way. It is always safe, it always holds out justified hope, never to be disappointed. There is no fear in this new life experience ever. But it cannot happen when it is pushed and forced. It happens exactly to the degree the unvolitional processes are no longer feared.

Man finds himself in the ironic position of, on the one hand, deeply yearning for the manifestations of these unvolitional processes and, on the other, fearing and battling against them. This is a terrible and a tragic conflict. It can only be resolved when the fear is given up. The yearning can only be fulfilled when the fear is given up.

All psychological problems come, in the final analysis, from this much deeper existential conflict, which goes far beyond the individual neuroses and the personal difficulties a child experiences and which later cause inner conflicts and misconceptions. All life tends to resolve this basic existential conflict. For this to happen, the individual, neurotic conflicts must be found, understood, and resolved. The self must learn to see and accept reality in himself, in others, in life. Honesty must prevail and the little cheating processes must stop. All the character defects must be removed. And when I say removed, I mean full acknowledgement and objective observation of them, without the individual plunging into despair, leading to denial of those defects. This in itself removes the defects infinitely more effectively than any other approach. In other words, it is not a question of first having to have removed the defects, so that then something else can happen. It is a question of being able to quietly see oneself in the defect. Then and then only is a person able to perceive the existential conflict between the ego and the universal consciousness.

This spontaneously manifesting universal consciousness has nothing to do with religious precepts of a removed deity, of a life beyond this physical life. These religious precepts are misinterpretations that have come into human existence as a result of sensing the truth of this quite immediately available universal life principle. When a person senses it and gropingly tries to convey this experience to those who are still in the conflict of the ego with the creative life principle, then misinterpretations—spiritual processes alienating man from the immediate self and from practical daily life—must follow.

A person who is frightened of these alienating processes must find a compromise between his yearning, the deep sense of the present possibilities available to him on the one hand, and his fear of them on the other. The compromise is every form of formalized religion that removes God from the self and from daily life; that splits man into a spiritual and a physical being; that removes total fulfillment from the now into a life after death. All such views and approaches to life are nothing but a compromise between what one senses could be and what one fears.

This fear goes beyond the individual, personal, neurotic fears that come into a person's inner life as a result of misconceptions and personally experienced traumas, which must become utterly conscious in order to be dethroned from the power they have over you. What is this basic fear of letting go of the outer ego, so as to let the universal processes unfold and carry you? The fear is the misunderstanding that giving up the ego means giving up existence. In order to get a little better understanding of this problem, let us consider some of the aspects of the process by which the ego formed itself out of universal life.

Individualization is an integral aspect of the universal life principle. Since life is always moving, reaching out, expanding and contracting, finding new areas of experience and branching into new boundaries, creative life finds forever new forms in which to experience itself. As I said before, if individualization separates itself further and further in its own consciousness from its original source, when it "forgets," so to speak, its essence and becomes oblivious of its own principles and laws, it seems a totally separate entity. Therefore, it is quite understandable that it can identify itself only as a separate entity. It can associate individual existence only with separate existence. Thus, giving up its ego must appear to it as annihilation of its own unique individuality.

This is the position of the human being. He lives under the illusion of being a separate existence and under the further illusion that only as a separate existence can life, the sense of "I am," be found. This illusion has brought death into the human realm, for death is nothing but this illusion being carried to its final absurdity.

The realization of the illusory character of separate ego existence is an extremely important step in the evolution of mankind. Any kind of self-realization brings this into very clear focus. To the extent you, as individuals, look at the immediately available truth of yourselves—all these apparently insignificant patterns and attitudes that seem to have nothing to do with such metaphysical concepts as I discuss here but yet are directly connected with them—to that degree will you find the reality that you and the creative life principle are one. You will then find that everything I say here is not merely a theoretical teaching that you can, at best, consider with your intellect. It is realizable and ascertainable right here and right now. The more you look at yourself in truth and shed the illusions about yourself, the more you will come into the reality that individual existence is not surrendered when the unvolitional processes of the creative life principle are allowed to take over and integrate with the ego functions.

Some of my friends have begun to experience the immediacy of this greater life in them more and more frequently. They experience a renewal of energy and find themselves in the apparently paradoxical position that the more they give of their energy, the more renewed energy is generated within. For that is the law of the universal life principle. The separated state is the dualistic way of life in which it seems "logical" that the more one gives the less one has and the more depleted one becomes. This is the result of the illusion that the outer ego is all there is to individuality. This is the root of the fear of letting go of all tight ego defenses.

By the same token, he who begins to experience these powers and energies also begins to notice, first only here and there but more and more steadily, the influx of an inspirational intelligence that seems to be much vaster than anything he knows of in his outer intellect, yet it is essentially his "best self." It first seems to be a foreign power, but it is not. It only seems so because these channels had been clogged up due to ignorance of their existence, due to not considering the possibility of their existence, due to personal little lies and self deceptions. This vaster intelligence manifests as inspiration, guidance, and a new form of intuition that comes not as a vague feeling, but in concise words, in definite knowledge, graspable and translatable into daily living.

The discovery of this new life reconciles the apparent opposites of being a unique individual and being at one with all others, being an integral part of a whole. These are no longer irreconcilable opposites, but interdependent facts. All such opposites, all apparently mutually exclusive alternatives that present so much heartache to man, begin to fall into place when the ego connects with universal life. When I speak of letting go of the ego, I do not mean its annihilation or even disregarding its importance or letting it fall by the wayside. I mean that the entity which has formed itself as a separated part of that universal life which is to be found deep within the self, immediately accessible if so desired, now connects itself back to its origin.

When the ego becomes strong enough to take the risk of trusting faculties other than its limited conscious ones, it will find a new security, hitherto undreamed of. The fear of this new step is generated by the idea that the ego will be crushed, that it will fall into nothingness and cease to exist. This fear is alleviated by holding on to unmoving, petrified psychic substances. The unmoving seems safe, the moving perilous. This is why life is feared, for life is eternally moving. When the moving is found to be safe because it carries you, you have found the only real security there is. All other security—trusting in and leaning on the static—is illusory and breeds forever more fear.

The principle of eternal movement is the same as that which moves the planets, which do not fall into space. At the core of the human predicament there always lies the feeling, "If I do not hold on to myself, I endanger myself." Many of my friends have become aware of it. And once you are conscious of it, you possess an important key, for you can consider the possibility that it is erroneous. There is nothing to fear, you cannot be crushed or annihilated. You can only be carried, as planets are carried in space.

As I so often say, mankind's state of consciousness at present creates the world it lives in, including the physical laws. Man is so used to putting effect first and cause later. This a result of his dualistic state of mind, which is unable to see the whole of the picture and always thinks in a split manner.

Man is not put into this sphere; this sphere with all it contains is an expression of the overall state of mind, the sum total of it. One of the physical laws expressing this state of consciousness is the law of gravity. It is a uniquely special law pertaining to this dualistic sphere of consciousness. The law of gravity parallels, or expresses on the physical level, the emotional reaction and the apprehension of falling and crashing when the ego is given up as the sole form of individual existence. Spheres of consciousness that have transcended the dualism of this plane have different physical laws corresponding to their overall consciousness. Human science, even from the merely materialistic point of view, shows this to be so. The science of space proves this; in outer space there is no gravity. It is not the last and only reality. This and many other such analogies are more than symbols. They are signs that could widen man's horizon in thinking and inwardly experiencing new boundaries of reality, thus diminishing his fear and his illusion of being only an isolated ego.

How are you to apply this, my friends, to where you are, most of you, in your search for your real self? This immediately connects with looking at the various layers of your consciousness. The more you succeed in making hitherto unconscious material conscious and consequently reorienting the faulty reflexes of previously unconscious material, the closer you come to the reality of the universal life principle in you. The universal life principle then becomes freer to disclose itself, and you become freer of fear, shame and prejudice so that you can open yourself up to experiencing it. Anyone can corroborate that the more courage is summoned to look at the truth of oneself, and nothing but the truth, the easier it becomes to connect with a vaster, safer, more blissful life within. The more connected you become with something that removes all uncertainty and all conflict, the more you will feel a security and an ability to function which you never knew could exist in you. These are functions of power, of energy, functions of intelligence that resolve all conflict and furnish solutions to hitherto apparently unsolvable problems. All ifs and buts in daily practical living begin to be removed—not through outer magical means, but through your increasing capacity to cope with everything that happens as an integral part and outcome of yourself. Moreover, you develop an increased ability to experience pleasure, as you are meant to do. To the extent man has disconnected himself, he must yearn for this potential way of living.

In connection with what I have just said, my friends, a peculiar phenomenon exists. A few years ago I used the following terms to describe certain overall, fundamental states of the human personality. First there is the higher self, which is what I have discussed here, the real potential in everyone, the fact of universal life in every human core. Second is the lower self, which is all man's deceits, all his character defects, all the illusions and pretenses, all his destructiveness and the way he secretly impairs his integrity, always hoping it does not count when he plays his little games that no one knows about, not even his outer consciousness. Then I discussed a third factor, which I first called the mask self and later the idealized self. This is the pretense that one is what one wants to be or what one feels one ought to be in order to be liked and approved of.

We have worked along in these years to come face to face with many aspects of this triad. At one time I spoke of a frequent phenomenon: man is often ashamed of his higher self, of the best in himself. I discussed then that for many personality types it seems shameful or embarrassing or humiliating to display one's best, one's most loving and generous impulses. For these character types it seems much easier to show their worst. It seems less embarrassing.

Today I can speak a little more about this topic, on a deeper and more subtle level. This is a very important point, immediately connected with the fear of and resistance to allowing the real self out into the open. What I discussed then merely described a certain phenomenon of certain personality types on a relatively superficial level. Although this phenomenon is related to and influenced by this deeper and more subtle phenomenon I want to discuss now, it is not exactly the same, for the specific personality type I then discussed feels shame primarily with regard to good qualities, with giving and loving. It appears to him that he gives in to society's demands and he thereby loses the integrity of his individuality. He fears his submission and his dependency on the good opinion of others and therefore feels ashamed of any genuine impulse to please others. Therefore, he feels more "himself" when he is hostile, aggressive, cruel.

What I wish to discuss now is that all human beings, regardless of their outer personality type, have a similar reaction to their real self, to the reality they are at this moment. This applies not only to their actual and genuine goodness, love, generosity, but also to all other feelings and ways of being. This is a strange shame, a feeling of embarrassment and exposure in regard to the way one really is. It feels as though one were nakedly exposing oneself. This experience can be registered by everyone and it is not the shame of one's deceits and dishonesties and destructiveness, nor of one's being compliant. It is a shame on an entirely different level, of a different quality. The only way I can describe it is that what one really is feels shamefully naked, regardless of whether it is good or bad.

This is extremely important to comprehend for it explains how artificial levels are created. These artificial levels are not exclusively a result of misconceptions in the usual sense. When the naked core of oneself, as one is now, is exposed, the personality is less frightened of annihilation or danger but more ashamed. The element of danger comes in when exclusive ego functioning is given up for the sake of non-volitional processes. The shame comes in when it is a question of being what one is, as one is now.

Because of this feeling, man pretends. It is again a different kind of pretense than the one that covers up lack of integrity, destructiveness, and cruelty. This kind of pretense, as mentioned before, is deeper, more subtle. Man may pretend the same things he actually feels. He may really feel love, but showing this real love feels naked so he creates a false love. He may really feel anger, but this real anger feels naked, so he creates false anger. He may really feel sadness, but feels mortified to acknowledge this sadness, even to himself. So he creates false sadness, which he can easily display to others. He may really experience pleasure, but this too is humiliating to expose so he creates false pleasure.

You will now understand the connecting link between this lecture and the one before, when I spoke of the artificial intensification and dramatization of emotions. This even applies to such elements as confusion and puzzlement. The real seems naked and exposed, so man creates a false substitute, often in the same area. Emotions are subtly falsified. This falsification seems to be a protective garment that no one but oneself—in his deepest, most of the time unconscious, self—knows of, but in fact, the "protective garment" anesthetizes him to the vibrancy and buoyancy of life. All such imitations build a screen between him and his life center. This also separates him from reality, for it is the reality of his being that he cannot stand and feels compelled to imitate, thereby counterfeiting his very existence. The moving life stream seems dangerous, not only as far as safety is concerned, but also as far as pride and dignity are concerned.

All this is stark and tragic illusion. As man can only find true safety when he unites with the source of all life in him, so he can only find his true dignity when he overcomes the shame of being real—whatever this may mean at the moment. Sometimes the fear of annihilation seems a lesser evil than the strange sense of shame and exposure of one's real being. When this shame is recognized and not pushed away as inconsequential, a tremendous step is taken, my friends. This is the key to a numbness of feeling that causes despair and frustration. It is the key to a particular brand of self-alienation and disconnectedness.

This is not translatable into rational language because there is nothing you can possibly say that distinguishes the real from the false in mere words. The words are the same for the real and the false—only the flavor of experience and the quality of being are different. The imitation feelings are often subtle; they are so deeply ingrained, they have become so much second nature that quite a bit of deeply sensitive letting go is required. Letting yourself be, and letting yourself feel, wanting to be discerning in what you discover, all this is necessary before you become acutely aware of the apparent exposure and nakedness the real feelings cause in you. The subtle imitation not only reproduces other or opposite feelings from those you register, but also and just as frequently, the identical ones. The next step is then the intensification, which serves as a form of substitute and as a measure to make the false appear real.

Everyone who first comes in contact with the universal life center he is can only do so when he is real—whatever this may mean now. Hence, before this experience is possible, he encounters this phenomenon of shame and nakedness. Meeting this momentary real self is far from "perfect." This is not a dramatic experience, yet it is a crucial point. For what you are now contains all the seeds, all the potentials, all the material you can ever need in order to live deeply and vibrantly. That which you are now is already this universal life power. Every conceivable power and possibility is contained in it. What you are now is not shameful because of your faults, it is much more shameful—or so it seems to you—in its immediate existential reality that seems so naked. When you have the courage to be that, then a new life, a new approach to your own inner life can begin after which all pretenses fall by the wayside. This applies to the obvious, noticeable and crude pretenses which usually can be seen by all but oneself and the subtle pretenses I just described. They stand between the ego and the universal self, forming a thin but firm screen that blocks out the life-giving force. They are responsible for the alienation from the universal life principle and create the apparently dangerous and unbridgeable chasm between the ego and universal power. They are responsible for this illusory fear and shame. This shame is just as basic as all the fears responsible for the misconceptions and the splitting up of the individuality. It creates its own fears and comes from some fears, but it is not exactly the same as the fears themselves.

The shame of one's nakedness in regard to one's self as it is now is the deep symbolism of the story of Adam and Eve. The nakedness of reality is paradise, for when that nakedness is no longer denied, a new blissful existence can begin—right here and now, not in another life in the beyond. But it takes some acclimatizing after one has become aware of the shame. It takes a path within the path in order to become more and more conscious of the subtleties involved here, and of the habit in which one is steeped in covering up one's inner nakedness. How easy it is to revert back to it out of long-standing habit! But once you pay attention to it and elicit the powers available in you again and again, so that you will notice your shame and your hiding and will learn to uncover yourself, you will finally step out of your protective shell and become more real. You will be the naked you, as you are now—not better than you are, not worse than you are, and also not different from the way you are. You will stop the imitation, the counterfeit feelings and ways of being, and venture out into the world the way you happen to be.

Are there any questions in connection with this lecture?

QUESTION: How can you determine whether your feelings are real or put on?

ANSWER: The only one who can determine it is yourself, by seriously probing and first of all considering the possibility that they may be put on. Do not be frightened of this. For man is terrified of the thought that his feelings are fake—be it in ever so subtle a way. He fears that if these feelings are not real then he has no feelings. He fears his own emptiness and this fear is devastating. It exerts a subtle pressure to go on pretending. But there is always a point inside where you say, "No, I do not want to feel." Whether this stems from childhood and personal traumatic experiences, or whether it connects with the deeper human problem applying to all individuals as discussed in this lecture, there must always be a determination not to feel. This determination is often totally unconscious, so that one is disconnected from it and helpless about the result which is, of course, no feelings. The terror is infinitely greater when the conscious self that wants feelings is ignorant of that side of the self which fears feelings. The terror of being unable to feel cannot be compared to any other. Therefore it is of enormous help to realize that no one has no feelings per se and that these feelings cannot ever die permanently. Life and feelings are one—where there is one, there must be the other even if one is inactivated at the moment. Knowing this makes it possible to set out on the search within: "Where have I decided not to feel?" The moment you become acutely aware of this, aware of your fear of feeling, you will cease to fear that you have no feelings. It is then possible to reactivate them with the help of reason, through realistic and rational evaluation of the circumstances.

Be blessed, every one of you. May your endeavors to become real, to have the apparently necessary courage to be nakedly real without any false covers, succeed. You cannot help but succeed if you really want it. Whoever does not move and grow and liberate himself does not want it—and it is important to know this and find the inner voice that refuses to move. May all your false layers fall away because this is what you want and decide. You will then discover the glory of living. Be in peace, be in God!

The Abyss of Illusion – Freedom and Self-Responsibility

G R E E T I N G S, my dearest friends. Blessed be this eveing, blessings for all of you.

You all know, my friends, that thoughts, feelings, attitudes and convictions create forms— forms that are just as real as your earth matter. The deeper and stronger a conviction is, the more lasting and substantial are these forms. These forms exist in your soul and they exist at the same time in the world of the spirit. If you harbor attitudes, opinions, convictions and emotions of truth and reality, these forms will exist in a world of light and they will, in your own soul, create and bring you happiness, harmony and what you might call luck. Soul forms of truth are made of "material" that lasts permanently. They will never dissolve, they can never be destroyed.

Convictions and emotions of untruth or unreality have the opposite effect. They may last a while, but their durability is limited by the length of time that these attitudes prevail in the personality. The stronger these convictions and attitudes, thoughts and emotions, the greater is their impact, the more substantial their form.

Some may remember that at times I have described the path you are taking by depicting landscapes as you know them on earth. There are shrubs and thickets, narrow edges and cliffs. At times the going is rough and tedious, the way is steep and stony. At other times, you find yourselves on a meadow of rest and light until you are ready to tackle the next hurdle. All this is not merely symbolic. These forms truly exist. They are the product of your inner attitudes and convictions, thoughts and emotions. Many of these create obstacles through which you have to grope your way.

The more unconscious such attitudes, convictions and erroneous conclusions are, the more powerful they are. This is logical, for anything that is out in the light of conscious awareness, if wrong, is open for correction. It is laid open for consideration and thereby made flexible and amenable to change. In your daily life you may experience happenings that change a conscious conviction. However, if you are unaware of a conclusion or attitude, it is not exposed and cannot be reconsidered and changed. It is rigid, and the more rigid a form, the stronger is its substance. If this is so with a form created from untruth, you will easily see that it must become a tremendous obstacle in your life. If you could but understand that all thoughts and emotions are actual forms, objects and things, you would better understand why it is so important for you to uncover your unconscious and look at what it contains.

These forms vary in substance, strength and shape according to what they represent, how strong the convictions are, and what is linked with them. This, in turn, depends on the character and temperament of the person.

Now I should like to discuss one common soul form which, to some degree, exists in every human being. I will call this the "abyss of illusion." There is an abyss in each one of you. This abyss is utterly unreal, and yet it seems very real as long as you have not taken the necessary steps to discover its illusory character.

When you cannot let go of your self-will—this does not mean that you necessarily want something bad or harmful—when you cannot accept the imperfection of this world, when you cannot have life and people according to your very own way, even though yours may be the right way, it seems to you that you have fallen into an abyss. You may never have translated these feelings into such terms. But, if you analyze your feelings, you will see that this is so. There is a strong fear in you that whatever happens that is contrary to your will means danger. Needless to say, this does not apply to everything and not to your entire personality, nor to all areas of your life. It is sufficient that it does exist in some respect.

By working in this direction and examining your emotional reactions to certain incidents, you will become aware of the abyss of illusion in you. I ask you not to take my word for it. Experience the truth of it!

This abyss varies in depth and width. Only by becoming aware of its existence and gradually discovering its unreality will this form dissolve, little by little. This can happen only if, at one time or another, you give yourself up to it. In other words, what seems so hard to yield to, what seems like a personal threat is really no threat at all. Let us say someone else does not accept you or acts in any way contrary to your expectation, or even the actual acceptance of your own inadequacy—none of this in itself is a threat. You cannot find out that this is not a threat unless you go through it. Only after accepting your own or the other's inadequacy in the areas where heretofore you could hardly do so, only after giving up your own will where it seemed as though your life were at stake, will you be able to truly convince yourself that nothing adverse happens to you. As long as this abyss exists in your soul, it seems to you that you are gravely endangered if you do give up or let go. In other words, you seem to fall down into the abyss. The abyss can only disappear if you let yourself sink into it. Then and then only will you learn that you do not crash and perish, but that you float beautifully. You will then see that what made you tense with fear and anxiety was as illusory as this abyss.

So I repeat: the abyss cannot disappear by itself. It can only vanish from your soul and your life if you have once made the plunge into it. The first time it may call for great effort on your part, but each time you try it anew it will be easier.

I hope I will not be misunderstood. I do not refer to giving up something needlessly, or merely because it makes you happy. I do not even refer to giving up something you have or possess. Nor do I speak of realistic fears that you can face up to constructively. I refer only to the subtle little fears in your soul, to the frustration and anxiety you cannot quite understand and for which you often find such poor rationalizations: when a person near you does not agree with you or has certain faults, you may feel all tense and full of anxiety. If you analyze these feelings, you will discover that it amounts to feeling endangered because your world of Utopia is proven unreal. This is the phantom fear which makes you believe your life is at stake. Otherwise you would not be so fearful. This is the abyss into which you should plunge in order to find yourself floating instead of perishing.

Last time I discussed the function of Utopia in the human personality. I said that the infant in you desires everything the way it wants it, how it wants it and when it wants it. But it goes further than that. This includes wanting complete freedom without responsibility. You may not be aware that you desire just this. But I am sure that by investigating some of your reactions and asking yourself what they truly mean, when you come to the root, you will undoubtedly find that this part of your being desires just that. You desire a benign authority above you who conducts your life in all ways as you desire it. You wish complete freedom in every way; you want to make independent decisions and choices. If these prove good, it is to your credit. However, you do not wish to be responsible for anything bad that happens. Then you refuse to see the connection between such a happening and your own actions and attitudes. You are so successful in covering up these connections that, after a time, it takes a great deal of effort indeed to bring the connection out into the open. This is so because you wish to make this authority responsible for the negative things only.

Many of my friends who are well advanced on this path will readily confirm that this part exists in them. If you follow through this unconscious thought or attitude, it amounts to just that: you wish freedom without self-responsibility. Thus, you wish a pampering, indulgent god, like a parent who spoils his child. If this god cannot be found—and of course he cannot—God becomes a monster in your eyes and you turn away from God altogether.

The same expectations you have of this god, you also project onto human beings, either onto a specific one or a group of human beings, or onto a philosophy, creed, teacher; it does not matter who or what. At any rate, the unconscious god-image you have worked to uncover will not be complete unless you include this very basic element in it.

It is of great importance that you find in yourself the part where you desire freedom without self-responsibility. With the method of our work, it should not be too difficult to find the many areas where you desire just that. It can go very far, although it is often hidden and can only be approached in an indirect way. I cannot show you now how it should be done, because the approach varies with each individual. I shall be glad to point out the way to each of you if you so desire. There cannot be a single exception. You all have this hope and desire at least in some way: freedom without self-responsibility to the full extent. You may wish to assume self-responsibility in some areas of your life, often in superficial and outer actions. But in the last and deepest and most important attitude towards life as a whole you still refuse it, yet you desire utter freedom.

If you think this through thoroughly, you will surely see that this is an impossibility. It is Utopia! You cannot be free and at the same time have no responsibility. In the measure that you shift responsibility from yourself, in that measure do you curtail your own freedom. You put yourself in slavery. It is as simple as that.

Even in the animal world you will observe the same law at work. A pet has no freedom but it is not responsible for obtaining its own food and shelter. A wild animal is free, or freer, but it is responsible to look out for itself. This must apply much more to humanity. Wherever you look, you will see that it cannot be otherwise: the more freedom, the more responsibility. If you do not desire responsibility to the degree of your capacity, you have to forfeit freedom. In a superficial way this applies to your choice of profession and to your choice of government, to practically everything. But where humanity has overlooked this basic truth is in the human soul and in man's attitude towards life.

The infant in you does not see this and does not want to see it. It wants it both ways. What it wants does not exist; it is illusion or Utopia. The price for illusion is extremely high. The more you want to evade paying the natural and fair price—in this case self-responsibility for freedom—the heavier the toll becomes. This, too, is unalterable law. The more you understand about the human soul, the more clearly you will observe this. All diseases of the soul are based on just that: evading payment of the rightful price, insistence on having it both ways, the easy way.

The price you pay is so heavy, so steep, my friends. You are not aware of this yet, but you will be if you follow this particular road. A part of this price is the constant effort you waste in trying to force life to fit the mold of your illusion in this respect. If you could but see all this inner emotional effort, you would shudder because this strength could be used quite differently. To let go of this illusion, to assume full self-responsibility, seems to you so hard that it becomes a good part of the abyss. You seem to think that you will fall right in if you really assume self-responsibility. Therefore, you constantly strain away from it, pushing against it, and this consumes strength.

Giving up the world of Utopia feels like the abyss. Utopia includes, among other things, the hope that freedom can exist without self-responsibility. Giving up Utopia seems to you the greatest danger. You resist it, with all the might of your spiritual muscles. You lean away from the abyss and thus lose valuable strength for nothing. It seems to you that to give up your Utopia is dire misery. The world becomes bleak and hopeless, with no chance for happiness. Your concept of happiness in this part of your unconscious mind means utter perfection in all ways. But all this is not true. To give up Utopia does not make for a bleak world. You need not despair over letting go of a desire and going into what often seems fearsome to you. The only way you can discover the illusion of this fear, this abyss, and its phantom quality, is first to visualize, feel and experience its existence in you in the various manifestations and reactions of your daily life and then jump into it. Otherwise it cannot dissolve.

There is a very important general misconception about life. It constitutes the main result of this unreasonable desire for freedom without self-responsibility. It is the idea that you can come to harm through the arbitrariness of the god-of-your-image, of life, or fate; or through the cruelty, the ignorance, and the selfishness of others. This fear is as illusory as the abyss. This fear can exist only because you deny your self-responsibility. Therefore, others have to be responsible. If you did not cling tenaciously to the Utopia of having freedom and refusing self-responsibility, you could easily perceive that you are, indeed, independent. You are the master of your life and fate; you—and no one else—create your own happiness and unhappiness. Observation of these manifold connections and chain reactions would automatically eliminate your fear of others, of becoming a victim. You could link up all unfavorable incidents with your own wrong attitudes, no matter how wrong the other person may be. His wrongness cannot affect you. This would become clear to you and you would then lose your fear of being helpless. You are helpless because you make yourself that way by trying to shift responsibility from yourself. So you see that fear is the heavy price you must pay for insisting on your Utopia.

In truth and reality you cannot possibly come to harm through any shortcomings or wrong actions of another person, no matter now much it may seem that way at first glance. He who judges on the surface will not find truth and reality. Many of you judge in some ways profoundly, going to the roots of things. In other ways, however, you are conditioned to judge on the surface. In this particular respect, many of you refuse to let go of judging on the surface because you still hope that Utopia can be a reality. Therefore, you have to fear other people, their judgment, their wrongdoings. In this part of your being, you like to consider yourself a victim for the very reason I stated previously. This trend in itself is a sign of refusal to accept self-responsibility.

If you are truly willing and prepared to accept full self-responsibility, the vision of truth will come to you: harm cannot come to you through others. I can foresee many questions coming up in this connection. But let me assure you my friends, that even a mass-disaster, of which there have been many in the history of humanity, will miraculously spare some and not others. This cannot be explained away either by coincidence or by the act of a monstrous god-of-your-image who favors a few and punishes some less fortunate creatures according to his whim or arbitrary liking. The God-concept is no less monstrous that says, "You were a good child, therefore I reward you by sparing you a difficult fate, while another person has to be tested and has to go through certain hardships." This, too, is a distortion of truth.

God is in you and that part of the Divine in you regulates things in such a wonderful way that all your wrong attitudes will come to the fore, most strongly at some times, less strongly at other times of your life. Due to the apparent faults and misdeeds of others, your own wrong attitudes and inner errors will be affected. But you cannot be affected by any wrongdoing or actions of other people if you do not have within yourself something that responds, as one note responds to another.

Again, you certainly should not take my word for it. Anyone on the path is bound to find out the truth if he or she really wants to. Sincerely investigate everyday occurrences, irritations, and annoyances. Find out what in you responds or corresponds either to a similar characteristic—although perhaps on a quite different plane—or to the exactly opposite extreme of a person who has provoked you. If you truly find the corresponding note in yourself, you will automatically cease to feel victimized. Although a part of you enjoys that, it is a doubtful joy. It weakens you and is bound to make you fearful. It enchains you utterly. By seeing the connection between your inner wrong currents and attitudes and an outer unwelcome occurrence, you will come face to face with your inadequacy, but instead of weakening you, this will make you strong and free.

You are so conditioned to the habit of going through life concentrating on the apparent wrongs of other persons that you feel victimized. You put blame left and right and thus never find the corresponding note in yourself. This explains how you could be adversely affected. Even those of my friends who have learned to investigate themselves with some degree of honesty often fail to do so in the most obvious everyday incidents. It takes training to condition yourself to follow this road all the way. When you discover your own contribution, no matter how subtle, to an unwelcome experience, you will cease being afraid of the world.

If your fear of life and the inadequacy of others is not to some degree eliminated after such findings, you have not even scratched the surface. You may have found some contributing factor, but if it has not the desired effect on you, you are still dealing with subterfuge. What you find must make the knowledge grow that you cannot be truly affected by others, that you are the master of your life. Therefore you need have no fear. In other words, your findings must make you see the truth and the significance of self-responsibility. In addition, self-responsibility will cease to be something to shy away from.

If this work is done in the right way, you will not feel guilty about it. In the right approach there is no room for guilt feelings. The very nature of a guilt feeling, which stifles your determined effort to find out more about yourself, is like saying, "I cannot help it, I have to feel guilty for something I cannot help." Therefore, inevitably, a guilt feeling contains an element of self-pity. Without self-pity, there could be no guilt feeling. The true and constructive way of searching within yourself must uncover many errors, many wrong conclusions, many faults and faulty attitudes. But you will encounter them without a trace of guilt. In the proper attitude, you accept your inadequacies and face up to them. In the world of Utopia you do not.

This is a good part of the reason why you reject self-responsibility.

By making independent decisions, you are bound to make mistakes. The child in you, clinging to the world of Utopia, believes you must never make a mistake. Making a mistake means falling into the abyss. Here again you can test the validity of your fear by jumping in and finding yourself afloat. You then see it is no tragedy to have made a mistake. The infant thinks you must perish if you do, and therefore thinks that no independent decisions must be made for which one is responsible. It should be noted that this may manifest only in a very hidden and subtle way.

Obviously, the illusion that you must be inadequate leads to your rejection of self-responsibility, and the continued wish to be free. The world of Utopia as well as the fearsome abyss of illusion therefore depend upon whether or not you learn to accept your inadequacy and whether or not you learn to free yourself of the phantom that you cannot err. The guilt and fear of making mistakes is so hard to bear that you set up all sorts of phantoms and soul-forms that make your life miserable.

In your intellect you may know all I say here, you may readily admit to a variety of faults without the slightest guilt or fear. In this particular respect you have freed yourself of the abyss of illusion and the world of Utopia. But there doubtless are areas where you do not feel in accord with your knowledge. With this we do have to be concerned. It is quite possible that you have some faults which are infinitely graver than others, and yet you do not have this feeling of shame and guilt. You can admit them to yourself, and even discuss them with others. Here you are free. Other faults, perhaps less severe and at times not even really faults but merely attitudes, a certain shame, a kind of anxiety or reaction, may give you an acute feeling of shame or guilt. You cannot face it, you look away, you struggle to avoid seeing it. This means that in this respect, for one reason or another, you live in your world of Utopia and therefore struggle against the abyss of illusion.

Your whole life must change in many ways if you discover the truth of what I say here. It is not sufficient that you accept these words intellectually; you have to experience them in yourself. This can only be done by hard work in the proper direction and by your utter will to find this particular truth. On the other hand, you need not have completely dissolved the abyss in order to be liberated to a large degree. It is sufficient that you see and observe its existence, its effect on you, and that you have made some attempts in the right direction. It is sufficient to see the connection between your erroneous attitudes and outer happenings that heretofore seemed arbitrary. Once you realize your fear of giving up Utopia with all its ramifications, you will have taken a tremendous step towards real freedom and true independence.

This will free you of your basic fear of life. It will release heretofore wasted forces for constructive purposes and it will bring forth in you a creativity you never dreamed possible. Once you realize what I say here, once it is your own and not superimposed knowledge, you will go through life with a completely new attitude: as a free being without fear. You will know, with that deep conviction that no word and no teaching can ever give you better than your own realization, that nothing can come your way that is not self-produced. You do not have to be ashamed of it. You can make any unfortunate circumstance a very constructive and productive medicine for yourself. This will serve to liberate you rather than to enslave you. You will realize that you have nothing to be afraid of. You are not the victim of others;

you do not have to fight for the perfection of others because their imperfection cannot harm you.

Some of you may think it is strange indeed that this basic spiritual truth has been so obscured throughout the ages. But there is a good reason for that, my friends. Humanity in its development was required to reach a certain basic spiritual understanding before it could use this knowledge in the right way. For, misunderstood, it could indeed be very harmful. If man's lower nature remains dominant, he might say, "I can kill and plunder and be as selfish as I want. My wrong actions cannot harm anyone else." And of course that is not true, not in the sense I mean. I realize, my friends, that this seems like an utter contradiction. I say here on the one hand that the wrongdoings of another person cannot harm you. I say on the other hand that if you go ahead, following your lowest instincts, it is harmful. Both are true, my friends, but both can be untrue, if you understand this in the wrong sense. It is extremely difficult for me to explain how these paradoxes hold true. However, I will on a future occasion attempt to make this clear, if you still need clarification. But I believe any of you who take this particular road on your path and experience the truth of my words personally, will know that both are true and that these two statements do not contradict each other at all.

There is just one thing I would like to add. First, it may appear that it has nothing to do with this paradox, yet, when you think more profoundly about it, you will clearly see that it has. I have often said, and many of you have experienced it, that your subconscious affects the subconscious of another person. This is so true and so apparent that all you have to do is open your eyes to have it constantly confirmed in your life. You know that the human personality consists of various levels or, expressed in a different way, of various subtle bodies. According to the level on which you give out, you affect that particular level of the other person. What comes out of your true being, your real self, will affect the real self of the other person. What comes out of any layer of your mask-self will affect the similar or corresponding mask-self or defense mechanism of the other person.

I will give you just one example at random that I am sure many of you have experienced. When you are shy and reticent, it creates in the other person a similar effect although he may express it in an entirely different manner. If you are not genuine or if you act out of a level of pride, the other person will respond automatically in kind. If you are spontaneous and genuine, you will find such immediate response in the other person. All you have to do is observe this. For that you have to observe yourself of course, in order to establish from what layer of your personality you have acted. Then only can you take the other person's behavior and mannerism and compare. You will soon stop being deceived by appearances. Your shyness may be open; the other person's shyness may be covered under a mask of brashness. However, you will recognize the same level. This is so important, my friends, and it has very much to do with the apparent paradox that you cannot be harmed by other people and yet it would be harmful to go ahead on that assumption and indulge in the lowest instincts.

Now, my friends, if there are any questions, I shall be glad to answer them.

QUESTION: A few times you mentioned guilt and shame. Couldn't one be ashamed of something without having guilt feelings?

ANSWER: Yes, of course. This is always a question of terminology. There is a healthy kind of shame that is constructive and strengthening. You can also call it repentance. If you recognize that you have unwillingly hurt others by one of your wrong tendencies and you feel truly sorry about it and this gives you incentive to change, it is good. If shame does not weaken you, but strengthens you, it contains no guilt. If it is free of self-pity, of the flavor of, "Poor me, I could not help it, I should be helped, people are unfair to me," then it is a healthy kind of repentance that has nothing whatever to do with guilt. So it is indeed possible for shame to exist without guilt. And it is also possible the other way around, namely that a person has an acute guilt feeling and is not necessarily ashamed.

I retire with my blessings for each and every one of you, my friends. The strength and the light I am allowed to bring from my world is flowing now to each one of you. May it help you, wherever you are on your path, whatever your problems are. May you feel the love with which we come to you. Be blessed, be in God.

Fear of Self—
Giving and Receiving

R E E T I N G S, my dearest friends. May this evening prove helpful and strengthening once again for all of you, and thus become the blessing that opens the further way on your path of self-realization.

In order to realize that which you truly are, the fundamental prerequisite is fearlessness. Every kind of fear amounts, in the last analysis, to fear of self. For if there were no fear of your own inner-most self, you could not possibly fear anything in life; therefore you could not fear death. Fear of self is the key. Before a human being enters on any intensive path of self-confrontation, he does not know that he really fears only his own unknown depths. He projects this real fear onto any number of outer and other fears of which he may or may not become aware in the course of his life, for these projected and displaced fears may be denied and covered up as well. A person may, for example, fear any specific aspect of living. All the power of his hidden fear of self may converge and concentrate on a certain fear or a few specific fears. Or life as such may be feared and thus avoided—as the self is avoided to the degree it is feared. This general fear of life may further be projected onto a fear of death—since they are really one and the same. He who fears the one must fear the other.

Only when this pathwork has become concentrated and awareness has sufficiently increased do you realize that you are really most afraid of yourself. You recognize this fear by the constraint with which you encounter yourself, by all the more or less obvious forms of resisting, by your terror of letting go of your defenses and allowing the expression of natural feelings.

The degree of guardedness and prohibition of spontaneity and naturalness is also not clear to you to begin with; these defenses have become so much second nature that you do not even know that they are unnatural and that you could be quite different. Your inability to let involuntary forces guide you is a sign that you distrust your innermost self.

In direct continuation of the last lecture, I wish to stress that anyone who constricts his natural soul movements does so because he is afraid of them—afraid of where they will lead him and what they may make him do. Anyone who is aware of this fear has made a substantial step toward liberation, for unless one is aware of the fear of self, it cannot be overcome.

Fear of letting go means that the real self cannot manifest since it can only be a spontaneous expression. Such spontaneity exists, for example, when knowledge manifests intuitively from within yourself, not through a learning process introduced from the outside. Only the person who is free of the fear of self, at least to some degree, can even register let alone summon the courage to acknowledge and follow through on such intuitive, spontaneous manifestations of the inner being. The great artists and the great scientists make their important discoveries through this process. In this particular respect, they must be unafraid of their inner self though in other respects they too may block it out.

The manifestation of the real self is always a profoundly creative process, whether as intuitive knowing or as the fullness and depth of feeling that make the personality vibrantly alive and joyous on all levels.

Fear of not conforming to the environment is another aspect of the fear of self. The inner reality may be at variance with the environment; the real values of the self may be different from the values of society. Only he who does not fear his inner self in this respect will refuse the ready-made values handed down to him. Outer values, whether right or wrong, are still shackles if they are not freely chosen.

One of the most important aspects of the fear of self is fear of pleasure. The entity is created for the purpose of experiencing pleasure supreme, intense joy, though the majority of individuals do not do so at all. The truly healthy and fulfilled individual who functions as he is meant to function according to his inborn capacities, can completely surrender to the life force as it manifests in him with its pleasure currents. He will spontaneously express this powerful force; he will not fear and reject it. This will enliven his entire system with beautiful strength, energy and delight.

He who is caught in guardedness and defensiveness and who is constantly watching himself so that these forces cannot express themselves, numbs himself to a greater or lesser degree. He becomes dead. The prevalent manifestation in this world, today no more than at other times, is what may be called self-alienation, or lack of aliveness, or disconnectedness. It is a deadness and brings in its wake a sense of emptiness and meaninglessness. It is deadness because the life force in its vibrant flow is willfully interrupted and prohibited by an overwatchful, denying attitude on the part of the outer ego.

The average human being experiences some aliveness at least at certain times, but is so inhibited in comparison to what he could be that the full aliveness, even if there were a way to describe it adequately in words, would sound unbelievable. Man does not even know how he could function and what his life could be like. He only has a vague longing, a vague sense that life could be different. Unfortunate is he who ascribes this longing to illusion, to lack of realism, and who then resigns himself to a half-dead life in the assumption that this is the way it must be. Fortunate is he who has the courage to acknowledge this longing, no matter how late in life, and then begins by allowing for the possibility that this longing is justified and means that much more can be had in life. And more can be had out of life if you become alive. And you can only become alive to the degree you overcome the fear of self.

Now let us consider this fear of self a little more closely, my friends. Why is a human being afraid that if he is not guarded and constantly watchful with his will and his mind, something dangerous might happen? This dangerous something would manifest from the spontaneous depth of his being. What is it? Fundamentally there are two possibilities, if we bring it to the lowest common denominator. There is the possibility that something negative and destructive would come out, and there is the possibility that something creative, constructive, expanding and pleasurable would come out. It is not true, as might offhand be believed, that only the former is feared. Fear of the negative is, of course, one very substantial reason for the constrictedness with which the individual prohibits free flowing soul movements, the cosmic flow as it manifests in each created human being if it is unhampered, unmanipulated, uninterfered with. The destructive forces which the individual fears may vary to every conceivable degree of hate, hostility, resentment, rage, anger, cruelty. They exist in every human being.

They exist to the degree to which positive expressions have been prohibited—first by the parents and the environment in the ignorant belief that these positive expressions are harmful and may lead to danger, and later by the individual himself. This is very important to understand, my friends: you are not prohibited, once you are an adult, by your past. You prohibit yourself when you continue to hold back those constructive forces which were originally forbidden by others.

Here, again, is one of those famous vicious circles that result from every error, every erroneous way of being. Because positive forces are restricted, negative forces grow. Or, to put it more accurately, the positive force is twisted, disturbed, converted, distorted, and thus becomes a negative one. It is not a different force that comes newly into existence, as you know. Rage is not a new emotion or energy current. It is of the same original substance that was love and can turn back into love if it is allowed to do so. In fact, it is easy for it to reconvert to its original manifestation, for this is its natural form. For example, once rage is admitted to exist and fully experienced in a way that is not destructive to anyone, under the proper circumstances and in a manner which at one and the same time lets one fully identify with the emotion and yet keep a sense of proportion about it—without rejecting the total personality because of it—the rage will transform itself into warmth, pleasure feelings, love. This transformation may occur directly or indirectly via a number of other emotions such as sadness, self-pity, pain, healthy aggression and self-assertion.

All these energy-currents must be experienced and owned up to, they must be allowed to exist at the moment and for as long as they naturally exist. Then and then only will that which is unnatural and destructive reconvert itself.

Now let us go back to the vicious circle, in which such a healthy procedure as the one outlined here is omitted: the greater the rage, the worse the fear of it becomes, and consequently the more the individual guards himself. The more he is guarded, the less is it possible for him to be spontaneous and thus to allow the destructive emotion to reconvert to its original pleasure-current.

As I said, not only the destructive forces are feared, but often love and pleasure are feared as much if not even more, because the child has been made to understand that they are wrong and dangerous. They are feared because they require an unguardedness based on trust of the spontaneous inner nature. Love forces can remain alive only when the self is totally un-afraid of itself. Giving up guardedness seems like annihilation because then the spontaneous inner nature, so different from the watchful ego, cooperates in the process of living. Without this cooperation, life becomes impover-ished, but the acceptance of this cooperation hinges on meeting that which is feared. Thus in the vicious circle the love forces are feared because they demand giving up the watchful, stilted, premeditative guardedness that makes all spontaneity impossible. Frustration and emptiness increase anger and rage, thus fear of self grows, and so on and so on.

This is the cycle in which those who are unable to make the decisive step to overcome their resistance to meeting their inner fears are caught. This is the one thing most individuals avoid like the plague. It does not suffice to acknowledge in a vague theoretical way the existence of some neg-ative feelings. It does not suffice to make abstractions about them. They must truly be lived through and dynamically experienced. This is inevitable and necessary and constitutes the facing of the self we are always talking about. Once this is undertaken, it proves not to be as difficult or dangerous as first anticipated. In fact, the relief and liberation, the coming to life is so real and wonderful that the hesitation seems foolish in retrospect. He who can bring himself to take this step is blessed indeed, for life begins to open up only then. It is necessary to let go and let what is there come out, what-ever the feeling may be.

I emphasize again to avoid all possible misunderstanding: this does not mean acting out negative feelings when one is in the grip of one's pent-up anger, which only comes back to the self in retaliation. What is meant is that these emotions must be felt and expressed in circumstances and under therapeutic supervision where they can cause no harm. In fact, the more the destructive feelings are acknowledged and the responsibility for them as-sumed, the less will the person be driven against his will and intention to act them out in his environment. Such acting out is usually excused by find-ing "reasons," or else the person is unaware of how much more strongly he feels than the situation warrants, which inevitably affects others whether or not he admits this to himself. The acting out that happens daily in every-one's life may not take violent forms, but it is all the more destructive in a devious and indirect way. This fact is not sufficiently appreciated and very much underestimated.

All this can be avoided if the full strength of a destructive feeling is directly expressed and lived through. The more totally this can be done, the more quickly the transformation into pleasure feelings will take place. What happens after this depends on the extent to which the person is able to experience pleasure feelings, which again depends on several factors, some of which we shall discuss.

Some of the foregoing is a reformulation that sheds a little more light on the nature of fear of self. As long as fear of self exists, freedom and fulfillment in one's life are impossible, my friends, absolutely impossible. It is so much better to acknowledge this fear of self, to own up to it and say, "Here is where I am at this moment, I cannot really let out whatever is in me, for whatever reason," rather than pushing it away and making believe you do not have this fear. In this case the fear of self makes itself known in indirect ways, which you continue to rationalize.

From here, my friends, we go a step further and look at another topic that is very important and directly connected with what I have just said. It will give you a new slant on certain processes of the inner life of man. Psychology has postulated for some time, and quite correctly so, that a human being's unmet need to receive creates damaging conditions in his psyche. Much emphasis has been given to this. As the body becomes thwarted when its needs are not met and it is not given the proper sustenance, so does the human soul become thwarted when its needs are not fulfilled and it is not given the sustenance on which it thrives—love, affection, warmth, acceptance of its own individuality. Both soul and body require pleasure; without it the person becomes crippled, his growth stunted.

It is true that the helpless child is dependent on receiving all its needs from others, from the outside world; however, far too little emphasis has been put on, and by far, too little attention given to the importance of giving out. The frustration resulting from not sufficiently receiving was overemphasized in the last decades, while the frustration of not sufficiently giving out was very much neglected. It was correctly postulated that he who did not receive enough in childhood would find it difficult to give of himself, but usually that was as far as it went. Healing the damage resulting from insufficient receiving can be much better accomplished when the individual realizes that he is not helpless about his past, that he contains energies with which a new balance can be established; but this can be done only when he comprehends the far worse pain and frustration which results when he does not give out what he has.

The over-emphasis of this one psychological aspect has created a generation of self-pitying people who go around in life bemoaning the fact that they have been shortchanged; that they have not received sufficiently in their childhood and that they have to continue as cripples. The ability to unfold and give forth always exists, once it is contemplated, once it is taken into consideration. Much more of the pain in man's inner life is the pain of withholding what one has to give, and much less is that of not having sufficiently received in the past. This is quite easy to understand when you think about it in a dispassionate way. If more and more accumulates of any substance, of any force, of anything, this over-abundance must create tension. The over-abundance exists, my friends, whether you know it or not, whether you constrict it and hold it back in your fear or not. Therefore many of you are pained at least as much as a result of not allowing yourself to give forth whatever it is you bemoan not having received and wish to receive from others.

The energy glow of these soul movements is a continuum; they are an ongoing process. In order to be healthy and fulfilled, you must cooperate by allowing this process to continue in a functional way, according to the laws of life which prescribe that the positive forces be given on to others and that you receive from others what they let flow into you.

Religion emphasizes the aspect of giving, preaching that giving love is more blessed than receiving it. It constantly stresses, in one form or another, the importance of loving—of giving love, of giving mercy, understanding, and other gifts of the spirit. Here the distortion was, and often still is, that love is a command, a pious command that is fulfilled through sacrifice. Then the image forms that to love means to impoverish oneself. Loving acquires the connotation of a self-sacrificing deprivation. If one does not suffer for loving and for the love of another by short-changing oneself in some fashion, it is not considered love.

The command to love becomes more of an abstraction and contains the threat of forcing upon the individual certain actions that go against his interests. Up to this day, many persons' unconscious concept of love is exactly this. No wonder that man fears to love, since it is represented as a pleasureless, sacrificial and depriving act that impoverishes the self for the sake of being "good" and of pleasing an authoritarian god. No wonder love is rejected since the pleasurable feelings it causes in the body are denied and accused of being sinful. One must then fear love doubly: one gives in to its spontaneous manifestation and it becomes "wicked," or one cuts out the very feeling that makes up its force and it becomes an unpleasant duty.

Mankind fluctuates between these two extremes: one either remains the greedy, selfish child, demanding to receive exclusively and not in the least disposed to giving out, or one strains into the false concept of love as described. Since each of these two alternatives proves undesirable, man usually changes back and forth, although the tendency to one extreme may be stronger.

Only when you look at yourself with great honesty and a great deal of discernment will you find both these distortions within yourself. Now, how can a healthy flow of giving and receiving be created when such concepts and faulty attitudes bar the way? The fear of self must exist in both instances, for the natural impulse, or the natural, spontaneous urge is to give out abundantly—as abundantly and generously as all of nature does! This applies to the most outer and material as well as to the most subtle level. The greater this natural generous giving out is, the less masochistic, suffering, self-depriving the personality must be. The more false giving by self-impoverishment and lack of self-assertion takes over, the less real generosity and spontaneous outflow can exist.

There are innumerable occasions in people's daily life when they stand at a point of decision whether to hold back the self or to give out. The issue itself may not be important, but the underlying attitude is. The question may be whether to hold on to one's old grudges, one's old separating ways that exclude others in resentment or censorship, or to allow a new spontaneous attitude to come forth from the depth of the self. The latter happens naturally, not by force; it sees new realities about the other person that make the holding of a grudge meaningless; it sees no shame or humiliation in giving up arrogant pride; it sees no "lack of character" in understanding and forgiving. Many such "little" incidents loosen up the block of withholding that causes more pain than any lack of receiving. From there it becomes easier and more and more natural to allow feelings of warmth to flow out. But at one point the self must make this choice: to remain in the old, excluding, restricting way, or to allow for a new strength from within—and follow it.

Needless to say, this point of decision must be noticed. It is never unconscious in the way of certain truly unconscious material. It is quite on the surface, only most people prefer to gloss over it and do not allow themselves to acknowledge this "time point of decision" about so many issues in daily living. When this point is acknowledged and truly faced up to, it may appear like a precipice. The new way may appear to be risky, the old, cold, separating way to be safe, although you all know with your mind that this cannot be true, that it does not make sense. Giving yourself to this apparently new inner force of giving out seems like going with a great unknown wave. You may even sense the joy and liberation of it, but still, perhaps even because of this, you fear its further implications. If you can let go and give up the destructive attitude whatever it may be, no matter how covertly it manifests outwardly, you institute an entirely new way of inner living. It is the healing you have sought and hoped for. This is the way it exists—no other way.

Even after you come to this point of observation, you will not be able to take the step immediately. You will dwell a while in this teetering position and observe quite clearly how you exclude yourself, how, by holding on, you restrict the cosmic forces within your soul and constrict the outgoing flow. When you observe yourself at this cusp, you become aware of the implications of both alternatives—the old destructive way with all its rigid formulations and pat answers, as well as the new vistas that open up. When you observe yourself for some time at this cusp, at this point of decision, and then do not pressure yourself but simply observe in fullness and know what each way means, you will finally become capable of letting go the old way that refuses life, love, feelings, happiness, unfolding, giving forth of what you have to give. At this moment you may not have strong feelings yet, but you will have a new understanding that includes others.

This new way grows steadily stronger, provided you do not stop the flow. The flowing movement is beautiful—it cannot be adequately described. It contains a wonderfully working mechanism of self-regulation that can be utterly trusted. To the degree you let go and give up a self-centered, selfish, self-pitying or self-destructive attitude, fear of self automatically and proportionately decreases. Something new begins to happen from within. The creative powers begin to work in their functional way. Thus, you will no longer thwart yourself. You will no longer inflict frustration and therefore pain upon yourself, because the immense pleasure of following this natural movement will fill your being. The pleasure of both giving and receiving will become possible.

For you cannot receive as long as you do not go this new way. You cannot possibly open yourself up for receiving when you remain in the old position of refusal and isolation. As long as you do not let go of the restrictions you impose on yourself, you not only make outgiving impossible, but you make receiving equally impossible. A vessel that is closed cannot be filled any more than it can be emptied. When you hold yourself tight and guarded, you do not protect yourself from any danger, and you also close yourself to all the healthy universal forces—those that could and should stream out of you, and that could and should stream into you.

Because guardedness impoverishes and deprives, the person inevitably becomes enraged. The average person finds himself in the preposterous predicament of holding himself tight and restricted, guarded and overwatchful, unable to be spontaneous, always determining with the mind and the will, never allowing the creative processes to manifest. Therefore he frustrates the tremendous need to be part of the creative process. He frustrates himself by withholding from himself the intense delight and pleasure of being in the flow of giving and receiving. It is not an esoteric, otherworldly pleasure, disconnected from the body; it must be physical pleasure as well. The irony in the situation is that then he resents the world for not giving to him. The world wants to give to him, and yet he can never see what is given him. He goes blindly through life resenting not having been given to and he does not even know quite what. He resents those most who really want to give to him and rejects their giving, thus depriving himself even more of that which he needs and which wants to flow into him. This would help him to give out so as to become part of the creative process again. In other words, he disconnects himself from the cosmic, creative flow of giving and receiving, the constant turnover, the constant movement that takes place in the life process.

Now, my friends, these words are not impractical philosophy, perhaps beautiful but not realizable in one's daily life. These words are of the most practical reality, applicable any moment you choose to do so: any moment you can observe yourself at some "point of decision," as I stated. The truth of this applies to all levels of your being—the physical, mental, emotional and spiritual—that is, to your total being. It is all one and the same.

The impoverishment man suffers from is totally self-inflicted because he cannot face that "moment" I was speaking of in which he refuses that which is given to him and that which wants to flow out of him. The new outflow wants to do away, once and for all, with that tight, constricted, resenting, destructive, enraged, rigid place from which you do not want to budge. Anyone who can find this place in himself and observe himself on the cusp has the best of chances. His good will to heal, to become free, may make him reach for the inner strength and resources to make and follow through on the decision for the new way. All fear of self will eventually vanish. The fear of the negativity in you will vanish as you express it under the proper circumstances, and as this fear vanishes, the next fear can be tackled—the fear of pleasure, the fear of happiness, the fear of fulfillment, the fear of being in the stream without constriction. You will then see that acclimatizing to happiness and pleasure is not as difficult as it first seems, when you wish to give forth what is in you. It is only unbearable as long as you want to receive only and do not wish to give.

He who is still hooked, consciously or unconsciously, on being in a receiving state, must fear fulfillment and pleasure. Not being aware of his predicament in its total significance and ramifications, he then complains against the world for leaving him unfulfilled. These complaints and resentments may take as many forms as there are human personalities. Many are not even aware of making such a general complaint against life; this, too, may be rationalized. It is part of your pathwork to discover it within yourself, to discover how resentful you become and how you refuse to budge from the negative position because you feel deprived.

You must feel deprived because you make it impossible for yourself to give out of your wealth and are therefore afraid of and closed against receiving. Thus you are doubly frustrated. Your refusal to let go of the negativity, the refusal to give of yourself, makes you unable to receive pleasure, delight, happiness—often even material success, which does not involve the emotions. The great joyousness that you sense exists must remain unattainable to you. You cannot tolerate it, it frightens you precisely because you are stuck on that spot where you simply want to soak in from others. It cannot work that way. All efforts to attain liberation and well-being have to deal equally with the frustration of not giving forth and that of not being able to receive.

My dearest friends, may these words open up the way for you that makes possible the transition you seek so ardently with one part of your nature, but still deny to yourself with another part. Perhaps they incite a spark in you so that you can see, and decide little by little to relinquish, all that bars the way to your destination. This destination is complete fulfillment and pleasure supreme. Be blessed, be in peace, be in God.

The Process of Meditation

R E E T I N G S, all my friends here. Love and blessings, help and inner strength is coming forth to sustain you and help you open up your innermost being. I hope you will continue and cultivate this, so that you bring to life your entire being—all levels of your being—creating wholeness.

In tonight's lecture I want to talk about meditation. Of course I have spoken about it many times before. I have mentioned that there are many aspects and approaches to meditation. Now the time is ripe to speak about this important topic in a more comprehensive way, to help you to use this activity more effectively and meaningfully. In order to really understand the dynamics, the meaning, and the process of meditation and hence to derive the maximum benefit from it, you must be clear about some psychic laws I have discussed elsewhere in these lectures.

One is that three fundamental layers of personality must be involved if meditation is to be truly effective: the conscious ego level, with all conscious knowing and willing; the unconscious egotistical child level, with all its ignorance, its destructiveness, its claims to omnipotence; and the supra-conscious universal self, with its superior wisdom, power, and love, and with its comprehensive understanding of the events in which a person is involved.

In effective meditation, the conscious ego-level activates both the unconscious, egotistical, destructive self and the supra-conscious, superior universal self. A constant interaction between these three levels must take place. In order to make this constant interaction possible, a tremendous amount of alertness, of wakefulness on the part of the conscious ego-self is required.

The conscious ego must be completely determined to allow the unconscious ego-self to reveal itself, to unfold, to manifest in awareness, to express itself. As I said before, this is neither as difficult nor as easy as it may seem. It is difficult exclusively, my friends, because of the fear of not being as perfect, as evolved, as good, as rational, as ideal as one wants to be and even pretends to be, so that the ego becomes almost convinced of it on the surface of consciousness. This surface conviction is constantly counteracted by the unconscious knowledge that it is not so, with the result that secretly the whole personality feels fraudulent and terrified of exposure. It is a significant sign of self-acceptance and growth when a human being is capable of allowing the egotistical, irrational, outrightly destructive child to manifest to consciousness, of acknowledging it and all its specific expressions. This alone will prevent a dangerous indirect manifestation of which the consciousness is not aware and with which it is not connected, so that undesirable results seem to come from outside. Hence, meditation must deal with this aspect if it is not to be a lopsided endeavor.

The egotistical infant's anti-social desires and claims, convictions and attitudes must be exposed in exact detail. It seems hard to accept that there is something in you that is so very different from the way you want to be and the way you think of yourself as being. Meditation must constantly encourage this self-revelation not only in a general way, but primarily regarding specific situations you are involved in daily which are unpleasant or unsatisfactory.

The conscious ego must reach down and say, "Whatever is in me, whatever is hidden that I ought to know about myself, whatever negativity and destructiveness there is, it should be out in the open; I want to see it. I commit myself to seeing it, regardless of the hurt to my vanity; I want to be aware of how I deliberately refuse to see my part and how I therefore overconcentrate on the wrongs of others." This is one direction of meditation.

The other direction must point toward the universal, higher self, which has powers that surpass the limitation of the conscious self. These higher powers should also be called upon for the purpose of exposing the destructive little self, so that resistance can be overcome. The ego-will alone may be incapable of accomplishing this. But the ego can and must meditate to request the higher powers to help. The universal consciousness should also be asked to help your consciousness understand the expressions of the destructive infant correctly, proportionately, without exaggeration, without losing a sense of reality in the opposite direction. A person can easily fluctuate from an outer self-aggrandizement to a hidden inner self-deprecation. When the destructive infant reveals itself, the person could fall prey to believing this destructive self to be the final, ultimate, sad reality. To give a full sense of reality surrounding the revelation of the egotistic infant, the guidance of the universal self must be constantly sought.

When the infant begins to express itself more freely because the ego allows it and receives it as an interested, open listener, as it were, collect this material for further study. What reveals itself should be explored as to further ramifications, origins, results. What underlying misconceptions are responsible for such overt self-destruction, hate, spite, malice, ruthless self-will? When misconceptions are recognized, guilt and self-hate diminish proportionately.

What are the results beyond the momentary satisfaction of giving in to these destructive impulses? When this is clearly worked out, the inner determination to be destructive weakens—again in proportion to the understanding of this particular cause and effect. When this part of the pathwork is glossed over and taken for granted without particular and exacting insight, the task is only half done. Meditation must deal with the entire problem, step by step. Again, the interaction must be threefold: the ego must initially want it and commit itself. It must reach in to expose the negative side. It must also ask for the help of the universal self. When the infant reveals itself, the ego should again ask for help from the universal self to strengthen the consciousness for further work: the exploration of the underlying misconceptions and the heavy price paid for them. The universal self must be allowed to help overcome the temptation to give in again and again to destructive impulses. Such giving in does not necessarily result in action, but manifests in emotional attitudes.

This important aspect of meditation requires a great deal of time, patience, perseverance, and determination. Remember at all times that wherever you are unfulfilled, wherever there are problems, wherever there is conflict in your life, you should not concentrate with woe on others or circumstances outside your control, but must reach into yourself and explore the causes imbedded at the level of your egocentric childish self. Meditation is an absolute prerequisite here: it means the gathering of yourself, the calm, quiet wanting of the truth of this particular circumstance, the truth about how you caused it—and then the quiet waiting for an answer. In this state of mind, peace will come to you even before you fully understand. This truthful approach to life will already give you a measure of the peace and self-respect that was lacking as long as you held others responsible for what you have to suffer. These principles were discussed before, but most of my friends do not actively use them in meditation as much as they might.

If this is cultivated, you will discover two aspects of yourself that you have never known: the highest universal powers will communicate themselves to you to help you discover the destructive ignorant side into which you need insight for purification and change. Through your willingness to accept the latter, the former will become more of a reality in you, which you will increasingly experience as your real self so that despair about being bad, weak, inadequate, must fall by the wayside.

Many people meditate, but they neglect the two-sidedness of the endeavor and therefore they miss out on integration. They may indeed actualize some of the universal powers which come into play wherever the personality is sufficiently free, positive, open, but the unfree, negative, closed areas are neglected and ignored. The actualized universal powers will not, by themselves, enforce integration with the undeveloped part of the self. The conscious ego self must decide for this integration and fight for it, otherwise the universal self cannot get through to the blocked off areas. Partial integration with the universal self may lead to even greater self-deception in that the consciousness is deluded by the actually existing partial integration with divine powers and becomes even more prone to overlook the neglected side. This makes for lopsided development.

The next step in meditation is to re-educate the destructive infant that is now no longer entirely unconscious. This infant with its false beliefs, its stubborn resistance, its spitefulness and murderous rage must be re-oriented. However, this re-education cannot take place unless you are fully aware of every aspect of this destructive infant's beliefs and attitudes. This is why the first part of meditation, the revealing, exploratory phase, is so fundamental. It goes without saying that this first phase is not something one gets over with, so that then the second and later the third phase can begin. It is not a sequential happening; the phases overlap. Exploration, understanding, and re-education often go hand in hand; at other times they must proceed separately. The feeling for this must be cultivated; no rules can be made which relieve you of the need to feel into yourself, to know what to use and when.

It is easy to look past that which is stagnant in you. Even if the first mediational approach is properly used and you are capable of seeing new aspects of the destructive child in you, the second part of the process may be neglected. An understanding of the causes and effects may not be worked through. Or perhaps the third aspect of re-education is not fully undertaken.

When you go through the whole process, a tremendous strengthening of your whole self takes place. Several things begin to happen within your personality, my friends. In the first place, the conscious ego-personality itself becomes stronger and healthier, stronger in a good, relaxed sense with more determination, awareness, meaningful directedness, and a greater power of concentration and one-pointedness in attention. Second, a much greater amount of self-acceptance and understanding of reality comes to be. Unreal self-hate and self-disgust go away. Equally unreal claims for specialness and perfection also go away. False spiritual pride and vanity as well as false self-humiliation and shame disappear. Through the steady activation of the higher powers, the self feels less and less forlorn, helpless, lost, hopeless, or empty. The sense of the whole universe in all its marvelous possibilities reveals itself from within, as the reality of this wider world shows the way to accept and change the destructive inner child.

This gradual change enables the person to accept all his feelings and let the energy flow through his being. When the small, petty, mean side is accepted without thinking that it is the total, final reality, the beauty, love, wisdom, and infinite power of the superior self becomes more of a reality. This power cannot lead to unrealistic arrogance, specialness, and self-idealization when you are constantly dealing with your little self. Such an attitude leads to balanced development, integration, and a deep, reassuring sense of one's own reality. Realistic, well-founded self-liking must be the result.

When seeing the truth in yourself and wanting and committing yourself to this truth becomes second nature, you detect an ugly side in you which you were hitherto too resistant to see. Simultaneously you also detect the great, universal, spiritual power that is in you and that in fact is you.

Paradoxical as it may seem, the more you can accept the mean little creature, the ignorant little infant in you, without losing your sense of self-worth, the more you will perceive the greatness of your innermost being, provided you truly do not use the discoveries about the little self to beat yourself down. The little self wants to seduce the conscious ego to stay within the narrow confines of neurotic self-beating, hopelessness, and morbid capitulation, which really always cover unexpressed hatred. The conscious ego must prevent this by using all its knowledge and resources. Observe this habit of self-beating, hopelessness, and capitulation in yourself and counteract it, not by pushing it underground again, but by using what you know, by talking to this part of yourself, by bringing to bear on it all the knowledge of your conscious ego. If this is not sufficient, then request the help of the powers beyond your consciousness.

Another important aspect of this process of getting to know both the lowest and the highest in you is that you realize the function and capacities, and also the limitations of the conscious ego. The function and capacities are the wanting, on the conscious level, with all your heart to see the full truth of both the lowest and the highest in you, wanting to change and give up destructiveness. The limitation is that the ego-consciousness cannot execute this alone and must turn for help and guidance toward the universal self and wait patiently—not doubtingly, impatiently, pushingly—with an open attitude about the way this help might manifest. The fewer preconceived notions one has, the faster help will come forth and be recognizable. Help from the universal consciousness may come in an entirely different manner than your concepts allow, and this might be an obstacle. An open, waiting, accepting, and positive attitude must also be adopted, though it may not be possible to do so immediately. Recognition of its absence can be made into a constructive acknowledgement of where the self is at the moment.

There are many, many different kinds of meditation. There is religious meditation which consists of reciting set prayers. There is meditation in which the main emphasis is put on increasing the powers of concentration. There is meditation in which spiritual laws are contemplated and thought through. There is meditation in which the ego is made totally passive and will-less and the divine allowed its own flux. These and other forms of meditation may have more or less value, but my suggestion to the friends who work with me is rather to use the available energy and time for confronting that part of the self that destroys happiness, fulfillment, and wholeness. One can never create the wholeness the entity truly aspires to, whether or not this aim is articulated, if this confrontation is bypassed. This approach includes giving voice to the recalcitrant aspect of the egotistical, destructive self that denies happiness, fulfillment and beauty for whatever reasons.

So far we have discussed three phases of the process of meditation: (1) recognition of the unconscious destructive egotistical self; (2) recognition of the underlying misconceptions, the causes and effects, the meaning and the price to be paid in regard to the present destructive attitudes; and (3) reorientation, re-education of the destructive part of the self. What I will say here must be taken with great care, otherwise the subtleties involved will not be communicated. Re-education might very easily be misunderstood and lead toward a renewed suppression or repression of the destructive part that is beginning to unfold. You have to take great care and consciously and deliberately want to avoid this, and still not allow the destructive part to engulf you. The best attitude toward the unfolding destructive part is one of detached observation, of unjudging, unharried acceptance. The more it unfolds, the more you must remind yourself that its truth, its attitudes are not the final ones, are not the only ones you have, are not the absolute, and above all, that you have the power inherent in you to change anything. The incentive to change may be lacking when you are not fully aware of the damage the destructive part of you is doing to your life when it goes unrecognized. It is therefore another important aspect of this phase of meditation to look deeply and widely for the indirect manifestations. How does unexpressed hate manifest in your life? Perhaps by feeling undeserving and afraid or by inhibiting your energies. This is but one example; all this must be explored.

Again, some repetitions are unavoidable for the sake of giving a whole, comprehensive picture. It is important here to realize and remind yourself that where there is life, there is constant change and fluctuation. There is constant movement, even if this movement is temporarily paralyzed: matter is paralyzed life-stuff. The frozen blocks of energy are momentarily hardened, immobilized life-stuff. This life-stuff can always be made to move again, but only consciousness can do it. For life-stuff is filled with consciousness as well as energy; whether this energy is momentarily blocked or frozen or whether this consciousness is momentarily dimmed does not matter. Meditation must mean, above all, that the part of you which is already conscious and moving is geared toward making blocked energy and dimmed consciousness moving and aware again. The best way to do this is to allow the frozen dim consciousness first of all to express itself. Here you need a receptive attitude, not an attitude that what comes forth may be devastating and catastrophic. The panicky attitude toward one's own unfolding destructive infant does more damage than the destructive infant itself. You must learn to listen to it, to take it in, to calmly receive its expressons, without hating yourself, without pushing it away. Only when such an attitude exists, can the understanding of its underlying factors come. Only then can the process of re-education begin.

The denying, panicky, frightened, self-rejecting, and perfection-demanding attitude man usually has makes every part of meditation impossible. It does not permit unfoldment; it does not permit exploration of the causes of what might be unfolded; it certainly does not permit re-education. When an accepting and understanding attitude exists, it becomes possible for the conscious ego to assert its benign dominion over the violently destructive and stagnant psychic matter. As I said many times, kindness, firmness, and deep determination to transform your own destructiveness must exist. You have to identify with the destructiveness and yet you have to be detached from it. You have to realize that it is you; you also have to realize that there is another part of you that can say the final word if you so choose. You have to widen the limitations of your conscious ego expressions by realizing that you can say at any moment, "I will be stronger than my destructiveness and not be hampered by it. I determine that my life will be at its best and fullest and that I will and can overcome the blocks in me that make me want to remain unhappy. This determination of mine will bring in the higher powers which will make me capable of experiencing more and more bliss because I can let go of the doubtful pleasure of being negative, which I now fully recognize." This is the task of the conscious ego. Then and then only can it also call into play the powers of guidance, wisdom, strength, and a new inner feeling of love and a sense of penetration by the universal self.

For re-education, the relationship of the three interactive levels must again exist just as it was necessary for making the destructive side conscious and for exploring its deeper meaning. Re-education depends on both the efforts of the conscious ego with its instructions to and dialogue with the ignorant child, and on the intervention and guidance of the universal, spiritual self. Each, in its own way, will effect the gradual maturing of this infant. The ego must determine its goal to change the consciousness of the negative inner child; it must want this and commit itself to it. It must know that this is its task. Full execution of this task is made possible by the influx of the spiritual aspect of the deeper personality, which must, again, be deliberately activated. The consciousness must be in a twofold attitude: one of activity in that it asserts its desire, its goal, to transform self-defeating aspects. It leads the dialogue and calmly but firmly instructs the ignorant child. The other is a more passive, patient waiting for the final, but always gradual, manifestations of the universal powers which bring about this inner change, the feelings leading to new, more resilient reactions, to good feeling where the feelings were negative or dead.

Rushing and pressuring the resisting part is as useless and ineffective as its direct refusal to budge. When the conscious ego does not recognize that there is a part of the self that actually refuses every step toward health, unfoldment, and the good life, a counter-active movement may be one of hurried, impatient pressures. Both derive from self-hate. When you feel yourself stymied and hopeless, it should be a sign for you to search for that part in you that says, "I do not wish to change, I do not wish to be constructive." Set out and find this voice. Use meditation here to explore and let the worst in you express itself.

You can see here, my friends, how expressing the negative part, exploring its meaning, cause and effect, and its re-education, must be an alternating and often simultaneous, constantly fluctuating effort. You can see how the three levels of interaction combine in the process of purification and integration. Meditation functions here as a constant voicing and articulation of what was hitherto not articulated. It is a threefold communication and confrontation: from the ego toward the destructive self, and from the ego toward the universal self, so that universal self affects both the ego and the destructive self. Your own sensitivity will grow day by day so that you can feel what is needed at any given point on your evolutionary path.

Each day brings forth new tasks, exciting tasks, beautiful tasks. This should not be approached in a spirit of "wanting to get it over with," as if only then can life begin—on the contrary. Doing this is living at its best. You may begin each meditation by asking yourself, "What do I really feel at this moment? About this or that issue? In what respect am I dissatisfied?

What is it I look away from?" You may request the universal spirit in you to help you find these particular answers. Then wait trustingly for what may unfold. Only when it unfolds can you have a direct confrontation, communication, or dialogue with it and ask it further questions, as well as instruct it. With patience and determination you can remold the distorted part, but only after it has fully expressed itself. You can re-form, reorient stagnant psychic energy with your willingness to be totally honest, totally constructive, loving and open. If you find an unwillingness in this regard, then that must be confronted, explored and re-educated.

This is the only meaningful way in which meditation can move your life toward the resolution of problems, towards growth and fulfillment and toward realizing your best potential. If you do this, my friends, the time will come when trusting life will no longer be a vague, faraway theory that you cannot put into personal action. Instead, your trust in life as well as self-love in the healthiest way will fill you more and more, and will be based on realistic considerations instead of wishful thinking.

The paradoxes and opposites that you constantly deal with in life will be reconciled. This is important particularly in connection with meditation on the threefold interaction within you. I would like to discuss a few of these important paradoxes. For instance, let us examine desire versus desirelessness. Both are spiritual aspects and spiritual realities. Only to the dualistic, separated mind do they seem like opposites, so that this mind becomes confused, not knowing what is "right" or "wrong."

There must be desire in a human being, for only as you desire can you come to the fourth aspect of meditation. This is the expansion of your conscious concepts to create new and better life substance, hence life experience. This is the creating I spoke about in previous lectures. If you do not desire a better state of being—more fulfillment—you will have no material to create and mold life-stuff. Visualization of a fuller state presupposes desire. These concepts must be fostered by the conscious ego and the help and intervention of the universal consciousness must play a part in the creation of a more expanded state.

If you see desire and desirelessness as mutually exclusive, you cannot grasp or feel the necessary attitude. Desire must exist in order for one to believe in new possibilities and unfold into greater states of fulfillment and self-expression. But if desire is tense, urgent, and contracted, it forms a block. Such desire implies, "I do not believe that it can be," which is, perhaps, the result of an underlying, "I really do not want it," because of misconceptions or unjustified fears or unwillingness to pay the price. Underlying denial creates too tense a desire. Thus a kind of desirelessness must exist, which could be expressed as, "I know I can and will have such and such, even if it is not realizable right now, in this or that form. I trust the universe and my own good will sufficiently that I can wait and I will strengthen myself along the way to cope with the temporary frustration of this desire."

What are the common denominators of healthy desire and healthy desirelessness that make meditation and indeed, all life-expression, real and beautiful? First, there is the absense of fear and the presence of trust. If you fear frustration, non-fulfillment and its consequences, the tension of your soul-movement will prohibit the fulfillment you want; eventually you will even give up all desire. Then desirelessness would be distorted, misunderstood, and wrong, due, in the final analysis, to the infantile belief that you will be annihilated if you do not have what you want. Hence you do not trust your ability to cope with non-fulfillment and you are inordinately frightened of it. So the vicious circle goes 'round. The fear induces a cramp and a denial of desire. These very subtle, obscure attitudes must be explored in your meditation, so that you can come to the fourth stage of meaningful meditation. In this stage you express your desire with confidence in your ability to cope with both non-fulfillment and fulfillment, and therefore in the universe that is able to yield to you what you long for. The obstacles on the way can be dealt with when you know the ultimate state of bliss will be yours anyway. Then desire and desirelessness will not be mutually exclusive opposites, but complementing attitudes.

It is similar with the apparent opposites of involvement and detachment. It seems paradoxical to postulate that both must exist in the healthy psyche: again there is this two-foldedness. If detachment is indifference because you are afraid to be involved and you are unwilling to risk pain and you are frightened of loving, then your detachment is a distortion of the real attitude. If involvement means merely an expression of a super-tense will, based on the infantile insistence on always having what you want immediately and unconditionally, then the healthy, productive form of involvement is inverted.

I will choose a third example of apparent opposites which make one comprehensive whole if not distorted. Let us take the inner attitudes of activity and passivity. On the dualistic level these two seem to be mutually exclusive. How can you be both active and passive in a harmonious way? The right inner interaction includes both these inner movements. For instance, meditation, as I explained it here, must include both positive and negative. You are active when you explore inner levels of consciousness; you are active when you commit yourself and struggle to recognize and overcome resistance; you are active when questioning yourself further to let the previously unadmitted destructive side express itself; you are active when you have a dialogue and re-educate the infantile, ignorant aspects of yourself; you are active when you use your ego-consciousness to activate the spiritual consciousness; you are active when you create a new concept of life-experience, replacing an old, limiting one. When the ego deals with both other "universes" to establish connection, you are active. But you must also learn to passively wait for the unfolding and expression of both these other levels. Then the right blend of activity and passivity exists. The universal powers cannot come to fruition in a human being unless both active and passive movements are present.

These are very important concepts to understand, to use, and to observe within yourself. Look to see where they are distorted and where they are functioning well. When the three-way interaction within yourself takes place, there is always a harmonious blend between desire and desirelessness; between involvement and detachment; between activity and passivity. When this happens, the destructive infant grows up. It is not killed or annihilated. It is not exorcised. Its frozen powers resolve themselves into live energy, which you will actually feel, my friends, as a new living force. This infant must not be slain. It must be instructed so that salvation can come to it; liberate it, bring it to growth. If you work toward this goal, you will steadily move closer to the unification of the ego-level in the universal self.

This is powerful material. Be blessed, be in peace; be in peace, be God.

Individual and Group Consciousness

GREETINGS. Blessed be this hour, blessed be every one of you, my beloved friends. Once again I am allowed to come to you through this channel and bring you what you need at this particular time, at this particular juncture on your path. This need may not always and in all instances be quite clear to you in your conscious mind. In other words, some of you may not immediately perceive why this particular lecture is just what you require at this point; only later may this become apparent. Others may immediately be touched by it and know exactly that this is what they need.

I will start, as many times before, with a general discussion of some cosmic realities, some philosophical premises, but once again you will see that they are of immediate practical value for you. At this period of your history it is often said and often noticed that the Aquarian Age, or the New Age is bringing in a new group consciousness. This consciousness manifests in many different ways. Groups are forming in new ways, as never before. Community life is also taking entirely new forms. All these developments are expressions of something deeper happening; it is not enough to simply see this occurrence out of context, as it were. It is very important for you to understand the dynamic, ongoing principle of the evolution of consciousness at work here. You need to gain an overall view, so that you can tune in and perceive the wider and deeper meaning of what is happening today in your time dimension.

Ever since human beings have incarnated, the emphasis in the evolution of consciousness has alternated between individuation and group consciousness. It is necessary to change this emphasis at different phases of mankind's development. At one period man needs to gather his energies into himself and concentrate all his faculties on his personal being. At other times or in other phases he needs to develop through his relationship to his surroundings. This alternation exists in an overall movement as well as in smaller cycles—both historically for the entity mankind and personally for the individual.

At each change of phase, a higher level of development is reached so that what was gained through the emphasis of, say, the concentration on individuation, can then further the group consciousness. And what is being learned in group relating during that phase furthers individual development. I will now give a brief and surely somewhat oversimplified picture of this.

At the dawn of mankind there were few human beings, living scattered over the earth. The individual was more or less alone. He fought against the elements and nature as best he could by himself. He was generally in a state of such fear that he could, at that stage, just barely cope with the fear of his environment and of nature, but he could not yet handle the fear of other human beings. Thus he lived in a more or less isolated state. This must not be taken completely literally, for he did live with relatively small family groups, or clans. Already then he understood to some degree that he needed others' cooperation to fight the enemy, whether the enemy was the elements, nature, beasts, or other clans. So even at this highly individualized period on the lowest scale the need to get along, to cooperate with others, existed. The lessons that were learned at this hardest stage at the dawn of mankind could then be brought into the following phase, enriching group consciousness.

At a later period, in historical times, population increased; man's ability to cope with the elements also grew due to his development; he learned to take care of himself more efficiently. It is then that the need arose to widen the scope of his relating with others. Thus group consciousness came to be emphasized. From family clans tribes came into existence. Man had to learn to get along with others, though he was not yet able to widen the span beyond a relatively small circle of his own clansmen. Later the span widened and from small groups larger groups, or nations, came into existence. But this happened after further alternations, after other phases of increased development of the individualization of consciousness. Even today mankind in general is not yet able or willing to get along with all human brothers and sisters inhabiting the earth. The old consciousness still makes for separation. But mankind is now ready for a new influx, so that those who resist the movement will experience a painful crisis, while those who follow it will experience unprecedented richness and blessing.

Let us now return to the second phase I discussed in this great cosmic movement. Group consciousness at this very early stage meant learning to get along with others. At this early phase of human development, getting along could best be learned for negative reasons: the fear of an enemy. As man's development proceeds further, getting along with others will no longer be due to fear and need, but to love and mutuality.

Group consciousness means finding the oneness between the self and others. In the early period of the development of consciousness this happened in a very primitive and superficial way. Nevertheless this stage had to be traversed. Consciousness had to learn this particular lesson of cooperating out of fear. For extended periods of history the individual existed within the tribe, finding security in it. He could find security only when he learned the lesson of getting along. Then the tribe would act out enmity, suspicion, negative aggression, not so much by fighting between individuals, although this too always exists within the tribe or the nation or the family, but mainly by going against other tribes. In this expression of negative aggression, loyalty to the same tribe, protection of the brother within the tribe had to be cultivated. So you can see, my friends, even the negative manifestations of lower development—hostility toward the other, warfare—can be and are used for the purpose of evolution, of development of consciousness.

As population increased and civilization advanced, this movement had to come to its next alternation in order for evolution to take its course. As you know, in more recent history—just a few hundred years ago—the emphasis began to move more toward the individual. Individualism became very important. This emphasis on the individual has increased in the course of recent years, decades and centuries. Man had learned certain lessons in bridging the gap from the self to the other, so now the emphasis had to be put again on the individual, on his individual rights, on his right to be himself: to be different, not to conform, to become more self-responsible.

This phase is now approaching its end. The importance of the individual is not diminishing, but the emphasis is shifting to group consciousness on a deeper level of reality. The principles that were previously learned on lower levels can now be applied to higher levels. The lessons that were recently learned in the phase of high individuation can now be brought into the new phase of the development of group consciousness.

Once again you see here the familiar spiral movement of creation that you detect so often in many individual forms, on your own path. The same spiral movement exists of course in the development of mankind as a whole. Always the spiral seems to go around in circles, yet if growth is real, these are not circles that repeat on the same level. They repeat on ever deeper or higher levels—however you wish to put it. The levels are higher in terms of development, deeper in terms of depth of consciousness.

In mankind's history the evolution of consciousness had to alternate, again and again, between the emphasis on individualism and the emphasis on group consciousness. What has been learned in one phase on mankind's path is brought over into the next phase. What was learned in the phase of individualism can then be utilized for better relating. For example, the more self-responsible you are, the more you contribute to the group. The more you can assert your rights and your individual needs, the less you need from and conform to the group, the freer will be your love and your ability to give to the group. Therefore you can receive more from it. For the self-sufficient person needs love and intimacy, closeness and warmth which are valid, legitimate requirements for happiness. The greater the individuation, the better the integration with the group consciousness will be. It is therefore a great mistake to think of this development as an either/or. There are those who believe that group living is contradictory to individuation, and there are those who see individualism as being separate and opposed to love and brotherhood. Both are wrong, as you can see from the foregoing.

There are many more such alternations, historically speaking, that I cannot go into at this time. Actually there is a spiral within the larger spiral. The spiral I discussed here is a fourfold alternation that holds true on an overall scale of the evolution of mankind. But within the fourfold alternation exists a smaller spiral movement in which subdivisions of many, many more such alternations exist. For instance, within the larger overall phase of either the individual or the group consciousness, constant smaller fluctuations of the same alternations take place. And within the secondary spiral movement exist many more spiral movements, lower subdivisions of the same alternation of individual and group consciousness. An entity is born many times within one overall phase that may last many hundreds or even thousands of years, but he, in his individual life, has the same alternations to go through. One incarnation may emphasize much more one facet, another the other. Even within the same incarnation, he goes through periods of his life in which he, whether he knows it or not, concentrates more on the one form of development and, later, more on the other.

For example, a small infant is almost entirely in the individual state. Do not believe there is no lesson learned in that phase. When he reaches school age, it is his first phase in this particular lifetime of learning how to get along. More such alternations occur duing his life, each fulfilling a purpose and presenting a lesson. This may be a third spiral within the larger spirals. There are periods where living alone fulfills an important function. At other periods living and being alone represent stagnation and a refusal to follow the organic movement. The same holds true about the reverse. There are periods in which group development is essential for the development of the individual and for the entity mankind as a whole. There are other periods in which staying within that framework represents stagnation. When the one or the other should apply cannot be generalized. Each has to be evaluated in terms of the person's own path. The only thing that can be generalized is the observation that when the personality follows the movement of his inner path, he will be in peace and joy; when he does not, he will be discontented and anxious.

Living with one other person in real intimacy can also come under the heading of group living, at least to some extent. Once again it can be so misleading to try to adjudge whether it is right or wrong to be alone or with others. It depends in what phase of all the intermingling spiral movements an individual finds himself. If you truly follow your path, you will know that what is at one time important and advisable may at a later period be stagnating and not advisable for you. So you have to be aware that no specific course of action is always right. There is a continuous movement.

When an entity—individual entities or the entity of the planet—is ready for an alternation, when its development approaches the changing point, there are always new strong energies released into the planet from higher spheres. This manifests on the inner plane as a strong movement. When this movement is halted by the ever existing tendency to stagnate, to not move, it creates a painful crisis. You may look at all the upheaval in your human history from this point of view. Most such periods were a manifestation of this principle. When the new movement is halted, what would express itself in a blessed, rich way, can manifest only in a distorted, therefore painful way. This is how the intrinsic positive reality is distorted into a negative one: by not feeling, not trusting, and following the course of the inner reality.

Let me give you a specific example of something that is happening today in your time on earth. Mankind as a whole is ready to approach a much deeper phase of group consciousness. Its natural manifestations, if followed, would be that nations would transform into one human government; religious differences would disappear because the One would be recognized as undifferentiated. The whole "group," mankind, would apply laws of brotherhood, justice and love to all, sharing the wealth of the earth. Thus new dispositions, new laws, new approaches would be instituted that would yield undreamed-of results—also on the outer level. The other would no longer be "the enemy." But since mankind by and large resists this natural development, those who follow it must, perforce, separate from those who do not. They create their own communities in which, more and more, this new spirit will manifest. In the meantime the great new movement, halted by the resisters, manifests in a distorted way. This is why you find today the regrettable manifestations of "group consciousness" in over-population, over-crowded cities, monopolies in which large groups master the masses and dictate laws and values. The self-alienated nature of over-crowded living and working, in which humanness yields to robotness, is a well-known manifestation considerably talked about in your world.

Those who are not connected—consciously or intuitively—with the movement and development of consciousness are regressive and try to halt the movement, fearing it and believing it to be bad. But this cannot really halt the movement. It hits a closed channel that is alien to its benign nature and thus creates the unhealthy conditions talked about before. The group becomes an amorphous mass. Instead of a group consisting of highly individuated members, a mass consciousness is at work that must not be confused with group consciousness. The halted movement of group consciousness expresses itself in large groups selfishly running the masses; big concerns in which all personal connection to others, to employers, to aspects of the work itself, is lacking. These and many more such manifestations in your modern life that I cannot possibly discuss now in detail or even enumerate, are not the result of overpopulation, but of halting the movement, of not feeling and following it. Overpopulation itself is one such manifestation. Modern man is a small cog in a big machine, depersonalized because he halted *both* movements: his own individuation and the development of group consciousness.

As the movement is blindly halted, feared, denied, so population increases; greater communities embody mass consciousness instead of group consciousness in urban and industrial life, disconnected from nature. As group consciousness distorts into mass consciousness, so does individual consciousness distort into separatism and alienation from the other.

If the movement is followed, if it is not obstructed by blind resistance, by fear of change, but is trusted and honestly accepted, then these negative manifestations will fall by the wayside. As for those who follow the movement, they will not be affected by the distortion of mass consciousness. They will create a new group consciousness. There is a great deal of difference in this, as you, my friends, can surely perceive now. Mass consciousness eliminates the individual, group consciousness honors and furthers him. Each individual is, of course, an integral part of the whole. The more fully you function as an individual, the more you have to add to the group. The less you are a full-fledged individual, the less can you add.

In the mass consciousness it is entirely different. Mass consciousness requires non-individuation, a blind following, conforming. The halting of the movement creates a perversion of what the movement would bring about if allowed to function by the consciousness that directs and, in the final analysis, determines the expression.

This is very important to understand, my friends. Within yourself, as well as within the consciousness of the entity mankind, group consciousness has definite gradations and categories. Let us say that there are three major phases of development in this respect. Mankind as a whole, and all individuals that are part of it, have gone through these three stages. They are also going through them on deeper, respectively higher levels of conscious organization, until total oneness with the All is achieved.

On the lowest scale you need the group because you are frightened, you are dependent, and because you are not yet able to be responsible for yourself. You do not yet have the ability to establish a channel to your own limitless creative potential. This phase can be likened to the infant that needs the mother.

But you often find that an individual has reached the point where he is ready to move into the next phase, in which he could be self-responsible and establish his own channel, but is unwilling to do so. I might say you have all found this on your path, within your lower self. Since the planet also has a lower self, there are factions of people who similarly resist. So you must differentiate between not being able and not being willing to take on selfhood, and not insist that others—parents or groups—give you the sustenance that only the divine self can give.

A person who uses the group as a crutch and substitute for individuation halts the movement as much as he who uses individualism as a cover for his inability to be intimate, to be open and undefended, and who therefore fears the group. Such a one will have a stake in confusing conformity and mass consciousness with group consciousness and will use the rightful arguments against mass consciousness to blot out the existence of group consciousness.

When the individual organically takes the step from needing the group to emancipation and self-responsibility, the pendulum may first swing slightly too much in the direction of individualism. In this state he will rebel against the group and deny its value. This rebellion you also find within you, and you now know that to the degree you deny autonomy, fear and distrust it and thus depend on others, to that exact degree do you dislike yourself and those on whom you depend. Thus you need to rebel. But if you proceed organically, that rebellion will not be an extended, acted out, blind period. For the rebellion will be recognized for what it is and the emphasis will be put on the self, rather than on those against whom one rebels. Then the individual learns to utilize his dormant divinity. He will unfold that dormant divinity. Yet he is still in a phase where his concentration has to be mainly on his individual process. This does not mean going into isolation—of course not. Help and reactions from others are always an integral part of this phase. Others and contact with others are always necessary. Others are the mirror that shows where the self is stuck; and the self, in its individuation process, deeply needs this mirroring, this awareness of its effects on others. But in this phase, the climate is of, and the emphasis is on, individuation.

Then again comes the next phase of development on a higher level of the group consciousness. It comes when the individual has found himself and is fully self-realized and can thus benefit from and give to the group without losing selfhood, autonomy and self-responsibility. He does not lose his "privacy," his right to be different, his need to express his uniqueness—quite the contrary. In the group that has become thus evolved, there is no conflict between those individual needs and the needs of the group as a whole. Group consciousness does not level off uniqueness, but furthers it. The group is no longer used as a crutch because the self cannot handle life, nor is the group an authority that one needs to rebel against. The group is truly an extended self in which one can function as a free agent. The highest organization of group consciousness is that within which each individual has found his autonomy.

In overall development the phases are never that clearly defined. They overlap. There are many spirals within the spiral, many movements within the movement. Yet the movement is not haphazard and chaotic but is an expression of such profound harmony and lawfulness in the larger scheme that the human consciousness can only sense it vaguely at best. So I would say to you my friends, that at this period of your history, mankind is ready for the individual autonomy that can form groups and for the group consciousness that becomes an entity in itself. Those who obstruct it distort the group consciousness into mass consciousness and individual consciousness into separatism. Those who follow it will create the new world, the life of the new age. Community living is springing up increasingly, and although it does not always express itself in its perfect form, it moves toward it so that it will blossom in the best sense.

Now, in your particular community, in your particular pathwork and movement, you will find each of these phases of human consciousness represented. Even the person who is, on the whole, sufficiently highly developed to form part of this new age community has areas within him that represent lower phases. You all know this and have been working with these aspects. You find that part in you where you desperately need others because you fear you are not enough and have not actualized your inner God. This does not mean that you should now separate yourself from the group, for alone you could hardly accomplish the task of development. But you need to be aware of your wish to misuse the group in order to avoid meeting yourself.

You also find that part in you that rebels against the group and wants to shun it because you fear exposure and rejection; you fear your need and your weakness, because you do not yet know how to function without the pretenses of your mask and your defensive games. Again this does not mean that you should now abandon all your individual needs and forms of self-expression and submerge yourself into an amorphous group organism. It merely means that you should see and pay attention and understand and proceed from there.

So even while all these aspects may still exist in you to some extent, this does not mean that you are not ready to become a fully autonomous individual that is part of the group, being enriched by it and enriching it. You can be the one who finds his privacy and his individualization totally intact and his group living and intimacy totally unhampered. In the course of your movement on this path, you will find the phases I mentioned; all of them are represented. They coexist within the soul and that has to be recognized. Most of you have already found your dependency, be it on family, be it on a mate, be it on the group; you first unconsciously, and later consciously, expect from the group that it do for you what you think you cannot, or will not do for yourself. You have also discovered that you become frightened and uncomfortable in the group and want to run from it, because of your expectations and demands on it, as well as because of the hidden guilt and shame of your lower self. So you turn against the group and rebel against it.

You are all perfectly well aware of these aspects. But you have exclusively applied them to the parental situation: you, as a child, still wanting to have a father and mother figure. This is true in very narrow terms, in terms of this life, in terms of looking at it from a purely psychological framework. But from a cosmic framework, this is true not only in regard to a set of parents, but in regard to a whole group which you endow with the power that you resist developing within yourself. You therefore go into the second phase: rebellion against the group, resenting it, avoiding it. You need to find that part in you too.

But I will say that many of you have lately become increasingly ready to go into the third phase where you find true self-responsibility, where you find your own inner strength, your autonomy, your own channel to the highest, where you indeed stand on your own two feet because you have within you what you need. Therefore you need not fear and rebel against the group. You no longer need the group in a debilitating way; you need the group out of love and a desire for mutual giving and receiving. You share and experience the struggle of growth and the joys of life, the pain and the pleasure of living, and you are grateful for this richness of life with others in which being together in no way infringes on your privacy, your uniqueness, your need to be by yourself. That kind of relating is the true intimacy of fulfillment.

This kind of relating must also exist for a couple in order for the one-to-one relationship to be truly fulfilling. If you use a mate because you do not wish to fend for yourself, the relationship becomes unbearable. By the same token, if you use a group because you feel frightened alone, you must simultaneously fear and hate that group.

The negative expressions vary in the different phases. One person will be more in touch with the fear and the need, and less in touch with the hate and the rebellion. He will be more in touch with the fear of life and therefore the need for the group, or the need for a mate. The hate for those one needs and depends on is more dormant in that state. With others the hate and fear of the group is predominant as is the desire to run from it, while the need and dependency are dormant. A false independence is then cultivated in which give and take cannot be learned, nor can flexibility and openness. This person continues to cultivate a rigid, inflexible attitude in which he thinks he can control everything within and around him. He cultivates an unyielding false selfhood.

All the phases of the alternation of individual and group consciousness exist not only on the planetary level, on the scale of the total evolution of the planet earth, of mankind as a whole; they exist within each human being. From this point of view it will become quite significant for you, my friends, to see where you are. To be aware of this is of great importance. It will be a map for you, another kind of map with which you can chart your way, in which you can find the mirror of an inner situation. Without this awareness it would be much harder for you to understand where you are, what you do, and what your reactions truly mean. You will come into a yet deeper understanding of the unitary principle of life, rather than the dualistic principle. I so often give you examples of this. In this particular instance, the dualistic principle of life proclaims that either individualism is "right" and group consciousness "wrong" or "bad" or vice versa. Each "wrong" is easily rationalized using the distorted form of its true expression.

In the unitary principle both have their function and both have a healthy, truthful expression, though both can have a perverted, distorted expression. So it is of utmost importance for you to see where you are in relation to the group; to probe into yourself with questions. Are you needful of the group? Are you afraid of being alone? Do you expect of the group that it do what you do not wish to do or believe you cannot do? The answer may not always apply to the group, it may apply to one other individual, but the principle remains the same. The moment you are fearful of your aloneness, you must also understand that relating to the other—be it one person or a group—will be as difficult as your aloneness. And only when your aloneness is no longer difficult, will group living or one-to-one living be a true unfoldment of joy.

You will then move into the new consciousness that spreads its wings, that is rich from within and therefore adds to what is without and that can also take in from without and return it back into the inner world. In a group that consists of predominantly autonomous individuals, the richness multiplies and compounds with almost incomprehensible speed. This is a phenomenon you in your work here begin to perceive. Those who are following this new stream will perceive it and do perceive it. Those who may be very active in this work, but are not yet within that stream, are blind to it. They are not able to differentiate between the healthy and the unhealthy attitude toward group and individual consciousness. They cannot perceive that healthy selfishness and unselfishness are two expressions of the same source. But those who are within that stream, who have first entered into that cosmic current that moves into a wider and wider field will know that the group will never eliminate what you call your privacy or the autonomy of your being. It will further it. It will further your independence as you further your autonomy. By doing so, you enrich the group as the group enriches you.

New communities, new living centers of the new consciousness are springing up on Earth. They will live this consciousness and manifest it increasingly; they will practice it. It is important that you be well aware of this principle and this possibility that is speedily ripening into a reality manifest on your earth plane. Thus you can follow the various spirals within you, knowing where you are and what you move toward. Yes, I know, all of you have worked and progressed sufficiently so that you are quite aware of the aspects that are under discussion here. But it is one thing to know about this as a condition that exists within the human personality, and it is another to understand it within the framework of a larger cosmic scheme—that this is indeed a meaningful manifestation of a cosmic movement that you are part of, that all of mankind was and is part of. Such understanding will not bring this new force to a halt so that it manifests negatively, but will enable you to go with it in the best possible way.

As I mentioned, in each new phase, on the threshold from one to the other, new energies are released. So this is not the first time in history that new energies have been released. Each period had its own newly released energies and consciousness streams brought into the inner consciousness of individual beings. But mankind has now reached a much higher potential of development and those who follow this potential will therefore be swept on by this inner movement as never before. So I say to you, before terminating this lecture, that if you wish, you can tune in on this force and truly use it for your transformation. In this respect you are not yet doing as much as you could do, although your progress individually and as a group is substantial. You do not yet tune in enough on this force that is operative in the whole of the universal consciousness and therefore also in you. You still cling to the belief that this or that problem or attitude cannot be changed. By doing this you not only make yourself unavailable to the new consciousness and this energy force that streams inside of you, but you also endanger yourself because then this force will reverse the process and bring you into a crisis that could be avoided.

The force is there, whether you use it consciously or not. If you use it consciously and wisely and follow it, go with it, it will bring you into undreamed-of unfoldment and enrichment. If you stem against it in blind fear and stubbornness, it will turn itself against you. This is the law. No evil force is doing it; it is only the not-allowed and not-accepted movement of the whole, the divine flow that is denied. Whether it is denied because of ignorance or stubbornness or whatever else, makes little difference. So I say to you, my friends, wake up further. You are in a wonderful process of awakening, wake up more, take yourself out of your numbness. Look at it, feel it, hear it—the force within you. It is the living Christ Force that can bring negative material, negative stagnant attitudes into an entirely new expression. Do not hug to you your negative thoughts and convictions. The force is there the moment you embrace it, the moment you turn to it, the moment you lift your face to it—allegorically, inwardly, symbolically. Lift your hands to it, allow it to affect you and go with it. So much has happened already in this respect. It can be activated for the wonderful unfoldment of your life—the life of every one of you.

Universal love is highly concentrated here at these hours of our meeting, so that you do not receive just words, important as the contents of these lectures are for you to understand and to work with; in these meetings, a very concentrated love force is penetrating and enveloping all here. Most of you who do not numb yourselves are indeed aware of this. You feel it and are enriched by it. So I say, open your inner eyes and ears and all your faculties of intuitive perception to soak in the force that is here, so that what your mind learns on the level of consciousness can become a vibrant truth— not just a cut-off intellectual understanding, but a lived, vibrant truth. You live and move and have your being in this love and in this truth at all times; it is only that most of the time you are not aware of it. What you have to learn is to know it, that is all. You are all blessed, my very beloved friends.

New Age Marriage

BLESSED ARE your lives, all your thoughts, strivings and endeavors my dearly beloved friends. Without your deep commitment to live up to your innate potential as a God-person, we could never fulfill our own tasks. So we depend on your truth and love as you depend on ours. We depend on your giving yourselves to the Creator as you depend on our giving ourselves to Him. Let this beautiful mutual work always be blessed anew in the name of the Lord, Jesus Christ.

His name would never elicit so much ambivalence and negativity if Divine Truth had not been so distorted in all areas, even as to His life on earth and in heaven. All great divine influxes lend themselves more to distortion than milder forms of creative manifestation. With the knowledge you have gained you can easily observe this in your life: the great spiritual forces contained in dynamic love are more feared, resisted, and maligned than lukewarm currents. This is the deepest reason why such stringent taboos existed regarding sexual love; why releasing the spiritual forces seems to be the most threatening and dangerous experience of all. These powers are by no means merely ethereal; they encompass all of the personality and certainly include the body. This is why the Christ Force, the Christ Consciousness, the Christ reality has suffered so much misunderstanding and strife.

It is true that these forces are so strong that an unpurified personality cannot bear them. To the degree that negativity and distortion exist in the mind and consciousness of an individual, these powerful currents must manifest as crisis, pain, and danger. Nonetheless, to be part of these forces and receptive to them is the deep longing of every soul.

The development of the institution of marriage is significant from this point of view. A deeper insight is now needed so that you can widen and deepen your own understanding of marriage and use this knowledge to articulate your longing. This is always the first step toward bringing what you long for into actuality.

During the many centuries of its existence, mankind has developed in many areas. Let us consider some aspects of this development within the last few centuries in regard to marriage. This will give you an idea of the movement until now, which will open your vision to the movement in the future. You will see the current attitude toward this institution with the larger picture in mind. History can be properly understood only when the spiritual meaning underlying earthly events is gleaned.

In the not too distant past, marriage was primarily an arrangement that served a number of functions, but the function of sharing, of love, of mutuality on all levels of the personality was served least of all. In fact, love, mutual sexual surrender and the profound exchange on dynamic energy levels was rejected and condemned. Marriage was supposed to be a financial and social contract to satisfy other personality functions and lower motives; financial and social advantages were of primary importance in marriage. What was more significant was the absolute conviction that these lower motives and reasons were morally right and virtuous. Men married women who brought a good dowry, women who raised men's social image. In other words, greed and pride were glamorized and endowed with righteousness.

Men considered themselves the superiors of women. Marrying a woman meant nothing more than acquiring a slave who obeyed the master of the house; who saw to it that the man received every comfort and convenience but made no demands for herself. In exchange for these services, which included being an object for man's mostly quite impersonal lust, the woman received material security. She had no other responsiblity in life than being an adequate object to her master. Of course you understand, my friends, that man's responsibility entailed much more than mere financial responsibility. Since woman was not considered a full fledged equal, morally she was barely responsible. In those centuries the reality of emotional and mental responsibility did not exist as a concept, but it certainly existed as a fact. Even without the awareness of the concept, men acknowledged this fact as far as other men were concerned, but totally negated it when dealing with women.

Obviously this was not only the result of man's distortion and negativity; it was just as much the result of a strongly imbedded intentionality in the woman's psyche. Woman refused self-responsibility on all levels for the longest time and therefore co-created the unequal relationship between the sexes.

Both sexes equally feared—and still fear—the powerful spiritual energies involved in the forces of love, eros and sex between man and woman. This power is the creative itself from which all that is manifest is made. This powerful current can be evoked by different methods and not only as a binding force between a man and a woman. It can be evoked through spiritual disciplines within an individual, by himself or herself. In that case, it merges the masculine and feminine principles and power currents within an individual soul.

The unpurified soul cannot stand this power current. To the degree unpurified soul substance festers in the personality, the power current has to be denied, suppressed and split. Sexuality that manifests without love, commitment, and respect is just such a split off, denied power current. Human beings who believe that pornographic or promiscuous sex is more pleasurable than the sexuality that streams from a unified wholeness and combines with love and spiritual union could not be more in error. The precise opposite is true. But the power of such sexuality is so strong that it cannot be borne by the soul that still lives partly in darkness.

Another human error is the belief that a decently married couple who are faithful to one another are necessarily beyond the stage of split-off sexuality. The typical marriage of former times which I described before was a complete expression of the suppression, repression, and denial of spiritual power currents. In the man this denial often manifested as an inability to experience strong sexual feelings for the woman whom he loved, honored and respected. Sometimes the unconscious fear of the power current is so strong that the split is total and a man finds himself unable to experience sexuality with a loved woman. In many cases, however, the split exists with one and the same woman. He can give relative honor and relative love to a woman whom he has married, in spite of deeming her inferior, but blot out her reality during the act of sexual union. This act can only be performed when the woman becomes a low object in the mind of the man. Pornographic sex can take place within the framework of the respectable marriage and is socially fully accepted.

For the woman, the denial of the unified power current manifested often in total denial of the sexual reality of her body. Whenever her sexuality manifested in spite of all attempts to deny it, she experienced it with guilt and shame.

Today the misunderstandings about sexual guilt and repression in your world are almost as great as ever. These repressions and denials, these guilts and false shames are not merely a result of social mores and bigoted influences, but are actually the product of the inability to carry the force of the fully unified power current, whose strength can only be borne by someone at least relatively liberated from negativity, fear, doubt, and destructiveness.

The strongly sexual person who experiences sexuality without love, without a deeply personal melting with a specifically chosen other, who chooses passing partners without heart and mind, who is promiscuous, is essentially no different from the moralist who is faithful to a wife with whom he engages in surreptitious mating as a marital duty. Both are afraid of the love-sex current that is unified through the power of eros, through the power of mutuality in soul development and commitment to each other, through personal purification.

The man-woman relationship of the past and the attitude toward the institution of marriage are a direct result of this fear of the unified love-sex current. Self-purification was practically non-existent for the average person, existing only in the churches to any important degree. But there again, the full power of the current was diminished by the edict of celibacy. True, some specially gifted and advanced individuals evoked this spiritual power through their own separated endeavors. The mystical ecstasy is nothing but the release of a spiritual power current in which God is experienced as a living and physical reality. This can also ideally happen through the melding of a man and a woman who are sufficiently free from fear, who follow together a path of self-purification. Their union will release this inner power current so that they will experience God in themselves and each other.

Before discussing this experience more, let us go back to the evolutionary stages of your history. The picture I painted about marriage is not a very attractive one. Marriage as it has existed for so long was truly a more sinful state than all the sins the moralists who perpetuated these standards condemned. These moralists directed the accusation of sin toward illicit sex, toward promiscuous or pornographic sex that could be outwardly identified. It is true that these acts indicate denial of the God-given unification of love and sexuality—of the greatest power current that is in itself an expression of the divine Presence.

In a certain sense this fear and denial is a symptom of the unpurified soul, the fallen spirit, if you will. But since you all also fulfill a task in the movement of return to the state of Godness, it is futile to rail against this fact. Those who do this are themselves fallen spirits, unpurified souls, and a part of this evolutionary movement. The appropriate attitude toward fear of the full power current is acceptance of this fact of life; a gentle training is needed so that the personality can gradually acclimatize itself to this high-powered force and bear it in comfort. Ecstasy can and will become comfortable as the soul grows in stature. This happens through a process of development over many many incarnations.

The real sinfulness of the attitude toward marriage which prevailed not long ago was the result of secondary guilt. Instead of admitting the fear of loving an equal, man had to put down the woman. Instead of admitting fear of loving an equal and experiencing the pleasure of sexuality, woman had to alienate herself from the man by making him the enemy. Instead of admitting that he feared an equal relationship, man had to make woman an object. Instead of admitting the fear of self-responsibility on all levels, woman made herself an object and then blamed man exclusively for this mutual creation. Both sexes denied the fear which might be called, in a much deeper sense, the primary guilt, a guilt that all mankind shares. But the denial of the fear caused secondary guilts. Some of these secondary guilts gave energy to impulses of the lower self. So material greed was fostered. Money, power, social advantages played into motives for choosing mates. Public images, appearance values, idealized self-images were nourished; pride and vanity were elevated into false moralistic values. If you consider the moral indignation, the moral self-righteousness of men and women toward those who deviated from the accepted standards, then you see the strength of secondary guilt. The mask-self did not even pretend to advocate something genuinely good and valuable. The mask-self claimed greed, calculating self-interest, prideful appearance values, and the mutual using of each other as the highest of moral standards. Such claims go way beyond ordinary hypocrisy. A hypocrisy so deep-rooted and so pernicious required a strong uprooting, otherwise the soul could not heal. It is important, my friends, for you to see the nature of the attitude toward marriage through many, many centuries. People marrying for love were the great exception.

The collective state of consciousness created these conditions in most marriages of the past. The same collective state of consciousness also created karmic conditions, prerequisites for specific guidance for ensuing reincarnations. For example, the antagonism that generally existed between men and women had to manifest specifically between individual men and women to a much greater degree than is the case now. So it was often "predestined" that two such individuals had to meet as prospective marriage partners. Their elders would arrange it. This kind of union gave the scope to bring out in each person general and specific negative feelings and attitudes which, having become conscious, became the basis for transformation. Thus, my friends, the "marriages made in heaven" were by no means always positive unions of love and affection, of attraction and respect. The negative mutuality between many, many individual men and women created the collective consciousness, created karmic conditions and also created the then existing standards of society.

In very recent times, consciousness made a great leap. Mankind has truly become ready to shed these old attitudes and create new conditions, new standards, new moral values. This can clearly be seen in your times by many drastic changes. The women's liberation movement, the sexual liberation movement, and a very different attitude toward marriage are clearly signs of a newly emerging consciousness. These manifestations must be viewed in the light of an overall evolutionary direction, otherwise you cannot really grasp the inner meaning of all these changes.

In all evolutionary movements the swinging pendulum tends to go from one extreme to another. This is at times inevitable, sometimes even desirable, provided the movement swings into an exaggerated direction only to a certain degree. But when the degree is greater than necessary or desirable, fanaticism and blindness develop in exactly the same way as they did at the opposite extreme. So, for example, the sexual freedom of today is a reaction to the shackles of former times. To a degree this is a necessary phase which individuals may have to experience temporarily until the wisdom of the new consciousness completes itself, and commitment to one mate is experienced as a freer, more liberated, and infinitely more desirable act than the uncommitted free-floating exchange of partners. The cycle had to move from the involuntary monogamous commitment—with accompanying limitations on personal unfoldment for both men and women—to an awakening to the debilitating effects of this attitude and a consequent libertinism and polygamous expression. From there the movement can proceed to a new groundedness in real inner freedom and independence that voluntarily chooses the monogamous commitment because it yields infinitely more satisfaction, gratification, and fulfillment.

A particularly pernicious aspect of the old attitude toward marriage was that the sexual need as well as the need for companionship was polluted by opportunistic, materialistic, and exploitative ends. Whenever one soul current is put secretly into the service of another, both become negative. If love, eros and sex were to be given their rightful place, then the real need for success, for respect from the community, for material abundance could function in a higher-self way. That this pollution and displacement was looked upon as if it were the morally more desirable attitude was even worse. Mankind had to break away from this distortion and a certain amount of upheaval became inevitable: the sexual revolution had to manifest at times in undesirable ways—but undesirable only when seen out of context. Of course the true lesson must be learned individually. This lesson is exactly what I am saying here. The old ways desperately need profound change. A new sexual expression and a joyful acceptance of the sexual drive has to emerge. At the same time, individual men and women need to understand the enormous importance of the wholeness of love, eros and sex; of affection and respect; of tenderness and passion; of trust and mutual partnership; of sharing and of helping each other. It must be understood that the committed relationship is not a moralized edict that deprives you of pleasure. Quite, quite the contrary is true. It must be understood that the power current evoked through a fusion between love, respect, passion, and sexuality is infinitely more ecstatic than the power any casual fusion could ever be. It is so powerful, in fact, that the very authorities against whom there is now so much rebellion have feared this combined current more than anyone. These authorities are not that far removed from him who allows himself to experience sexuality only in a split-off way—cut off from the heart, removed from real intimacy and sharing.

Knowing the state into which you can grow, into which you must eventually grow because this is your innate destiny, is important. It is the blueprint without which you cannot steer your ship. But there is a subtle and yet distinct difference between this model and forceful attempts to be what you have not yet organically grown to be. If you recognize the model without forcing yourself, you accept your human state. You know that by virtue of your humanness you cannot immediately be the ideal, totally fused individual. You know that it takes a long time, much experience, many lessons, many trials and errors, untold incarnations until your soul substance has emerged to become this whole being. You need to know that such a state exists, even if you are still quite unable to experience it. You need to know it without self-pressure, without self-moralizing, without discouragement. All of these attitudes are destructive and erroneous.

The attempt to prescribe ideal standards that individuals cannot possibly live up to at this time has unfortunately been made by almost all of organized religion. This is why organized religion has fallen into ill repute today. The state of wholeness should be placed lightly into your consciousness, if I may use this expression. It should never become a whip. It should merely be a reminder of who you essentially are already and who you will one day become.

Just as it is foolish to turn into an atheist because of the errors of religion, so it is foolish to discard marriage altogether because of previous distortions. Before many different individuals began to question whether marriage was a valid institution the attitude toward this institution had already begun to change considerably. This happened in the last several decades. As opposed to the past, individuals chose partners freely, and generally were motivated by love. However, this also often led to errors. Only too often, individuals who were too young and immature to form a really meaningful union chose marriage based on superficial attraction and without deeper knowledge of self and the other. No wonder that such marriages could not survive. But this step, too, had to be gone through before maturity could be gained. As individuals cannot learn unless they experience mistakes and immaturities, so it is with collective consciousness. New ways have to be tried out by both before the soul reaches wisdom and truth. The freedom to choose independently, the freedom to experience sexual and erotic pleasures, the freedom to make mistakes and learn from them, the freedom to grow into different and more mature relationships along with the growth of the self without condemnation—all these are necessary prerequisites to learning the real significance of marriage. This means seeing it not as a shackle imposed by a moralizing outer or inner authority, but as a freely chosen gift, the greatest, most desirable state imaginable, the keenest pleasure and fulfillment, for which the soul and the personality have to become strong, resilient, mature and capable of carrying the power of its energies. Bliss, ecstasy, pleasure supreme can never exist gratuitously, can never be cheaply snatched. They cannot be borne that way. They can only be borne when the personality has reached sufficient purification, security, faith, self-knowledge, comprehension of the universe, Christness.

Sexual liberation has to go through some stages that may seem exaggerated, or may even be exaggerated, before further sexual liberation—the unification of love, eros and sex—can create the new age marriage.

Fleeting sexual encounters should not be looked upon as the final state of liberation. They are, at best, a very temporary and limited phase to go through. No one who has ever experienced this stage has ever truly been satisfied by it, not even on the merely physical level. You may delude yourself thinking that this is the best you could hope to experience, but it is not. You may deny your deeper unfulfilled longing because some of the hitherto unfulfilled longing has been assuaged. But you have so much further to go in order to give yourself what you really need, want, desire, and what you should indeed have.

As with the sexual revolution, feminine liberation too had to go into some kind of extreme—at least temporarily. So some women had to become as hard, as unyielding as their greatest enemy, the man, in order to experience their strength, their capacity to be independent, self-responsible, creative, and resourceful. As long as this is a temporary manifestation, a passing phase, an interim phase from which further changes will emerge, it is all right. But when this is seen as the final ideal, it becomes as damaging as the suppressed and dependent child-woman you no longer want or need to be. The new age woman combines independence, self-responsibility, full-fledged adulthood with the softness and yieldingness that was previously associated exclusively with the dependent parasite. The new age man combines his heart feelings, his softness, his gentleness with his strength and abilities, not in a way similar to the woman, but in a complementary way. The two can form the new age marriage.

The new age marriage will not be formed early in life. If the participants are young, they will have reached considerable maturity as a result of genuine, intense pathwork such as this. The new age marriage is a nucleus of strength, with the partners fortifying each other in their common voyage and also fortifying others in a commonly undertaken task for the greater cause. The new age marriage is totally open and transparent. There are no secrets whatever. The soul process of the pathwork is totally shared. This openness and transparency has to be learned. It is a path within the path, as it were. You need to expose your difficulty in achieving this openness rather than denying or hiding it. If you do not expose your difficulty in being open, your unfulfillment cannot be alleviated no matter how much you try to blame it on your partner or on outer circumstances. Part of this openness is revealing your fear of the strong spiritual current, of the forces released by the unification of sexuality and the heart. When the fear is shared—even though both may be unable to dissolve fear as yet—the obstructions will be eliminated relatively fast and a kind of vibrant fulfillment comes even from this sharing.

In the new age marriage a path of profound self-development and the emptying out of all hidden areas of the self is a prerequisite for fulfillment and for keeping the relationship alive. When the vibrancy ebbs away, this too needs to be met and explored by both partners together. There may be any number of reasons, none of them necessarily bad or shameful.

When all levels of the personality meet, join, are open to each other and finally fuse, the intensity and vibrancy of the sexual encounter will surpass anything you can at present imagine. You deeply long for this, because this fulfillment is your birthright and your destiny. It can only exist in a partnership such as I outline here: in the new age marriage. This kind of fusion cannot come about easily. It is the result of infinite patience, growth, change, transformation. But it should live in your vision as a possibility you can indeed actualize one day.

The fusion on all levels of the personality means the fusion of all energy bodies. This is very rarely the case. You will come to know when the fusion exists only on the physical level, when on the emotional, the mental, and spiritual levels. All these energy bodies exist as reality and can fuse, or not fuse, according to prevailing conditions. When the fusion takes place on all these levels, you not only become one with your partner, but with God. You realize God in the mate and God in yourself. No wonder that the power current is too strong to bear unless your personalities have reached a high degree of inner development and purification.

When it is realized that sexual fusion is insufficient and uninteresting unless it includes all the energy bodies in the process of coming together, the approach to a sexual encounter will be very different from what it is now. It will never be casual or haphazard. It will be considered a holy ritual. These rituals will be created by the individual couples and may change at different phases. They will never deteriorate into fixed routines. The sexual encounter is a true fusion of the masculine and feminine principles as universal forces. Each sexual fusion will be a creative act, creating new spiritual forms, new heights of development in the two selves that can be given on to others. The merging and complementing of these two divine aspects—the feminine and masculine forces—will create, not only total fulfillment, ecstasy and bliss, but enduring new values and a true experience of divine reality, of the Christ in the self and in the other.

My beloved friends, this lecture should by no means discourage you, no matter how far away you may seem to be from the possibility and the destiny I outline here. You are moving in this direction, merely by being able to comprehend this lecture, by being capable of choosing to use it in the most positive way, no matter where you are. Knowing this truth will free you as any other truth must free you, even if you cannot attain its realization in this life. Rejoice that it exists, that it waits for you. Know this truth as the enrichment which has been given you.

There exists a tremendous tension between the male and female energy currents. This tension can manifest in a positive or a negative way. If it manifests negatively, sexuality is hooked up with denial—homosexuality, repression, asexuality, impotence, frigidity—or with negative expression (sadism, masochism, fetishism). To a degree, it may be necessary to give some expression to negatively connected sexuality, for if it is completely denied, the total personality is being thwarted and the tension is so powerfully accumulated that non-sexual violence accrues. If these expressions occur in fantasy or in situations of mutual consent where no one is harmed or forced, they can be a step toward a more cohesive, connected sexuality, especially when this is not glorified but understood in its true meaning.

When the tension manifests positively, it is truly a psychic nuclear point. New age marriage is a psychic nuclear point. The energy released, the creativity liberated, the mutuality of ecstasy—these are deeply spiritual experiences, in, through, and with God. Divine sexuality must be recognized in the new age. It is neither to be found in the old taboos and denials, nor in the moralizing judgment about this creative force, nor is it to be found in the deviations that occur by necessity as a result of incomplete development. The explosive force of the male/female tension and its release mechanism permeates the total personality and transcends the finite. It truly spiritualizes the body and materializes the spirit which is the task of evolution.

With this, I bless you, my beloved ones. The Christ within your deepest soul fuses with the Christ Consciousness and energies that surround you and fills you with His love, His strength and His blessings.

Creative Emptiness

MY MOST beloved friends, blessings for everyone of you here. A golden force is flowing through your inner being now and forever, if you so wish; if you open yourself to it. I spoke to you in the last lecture about the coming of a new era. This requires that many, many human beings are ready for this spiritual event. For many years, you on this path have worked for that purpose, whether or not you were aware of it. You have filed away impurities and you still do so. You have made yourselves available for a powerful force that has been released in the universe—in the inner universe.

As I have said before, many spiritual teachers and channels know this. But many misinterpret this event. They believe that it will bring geological cataclysms with effects on the human level. I have said before that this is not true. The changes that are occurring, that are already in progress, are changes in consciousness. And you are working at this. You see, as you evolve and develop and purify yourself, you become more and more ready for an inner enlightenment and awakening that has not occurred before and that is self-perpetuating in its force. It is unprecedented for there has been no other time in mankind's history when this power was as available as it is now. What you increasingly experience is the result of this power's coming upon a receptive channel. This is what we must be concerned with, for if this power hits an unreceptive channel, crisis arises, as you also well know. Even if only a part of you blocks great creative, beneficial forces that could make you thrive in an entirely new way, you put yourself under great psychic, emotional, and spiritual stress. This must be avoided.

So on your path, you have learned to contact more and more those deeper levels of intentionality where you deny truth and love and a greater knowing and a greater power that operates differently from the outer ego power you so strive for. Real truth and love, real knowing and power, come from within.

In tonight's lecture I am going to speak about the importance of being receptive to this force, this energy, this new consciousness: the Christ Consciousness that seeks to spread and is spreading through human consciousness wherever this is possible. In order to do this, you also need to understand another principle, and that is the principle of creative emptiness.

Most human beings create an agitated mind, an over-activity of the thinking processes, an inner and outer over-activity, because they are basically frightened of the possibility that they may be empty, that there may be nothing within to sustain them. This thought is rarely conscious, but on a path such as this, the time comes when you become conscious of this thought. Then the first reaction is very often, "I do not even want to acknowledge that I am afraid of this. I'd rather continue busying my mind in order not to face this terror that I am nothing inside, that I am but a shell that needs sustenance from without and that needs to deny this fearful knowledge."

This is obviously a futile course of total self-deception. It is of utmost importance that you face this fear and deal with it openly. You need to create an atmosphere and a climate within yourself in which you allow this emptiness to exist. Otherwise you live in a perpetually self-deceiving way that is also wasteful, because the fear is unjustified. How can you ever live in peace with yourself if you do not know what you fear, and if you therefore make it impossible to find out that what you fear is not so?

As a result of a continuous process over centuries and centuries of your existence, you have conditioned yourself to make the outer mind a very busy place, so that when busyness ceases temporarily, the resulting quiet is confused with emptiness. It indeed seems empty. The noise must recede and you must embrace and welcome the emptiness as the most important prerequisite and channel through which to receive your innermost Godself.

Let me put it this way: if you cannot let yourself be empty, you can never be filled. Out of the emptiness a new fullness will arise, yet you cannot disregard and deny and step over your fear of emptiness. It must, like everything else, be gone through. My advice here is that you challenge that belief and at the same time welcome the emptiness as the doorway to your divinity.

There are several psychic and spiritual laws which you need to comprehend in order to nurture this emptiness and make out of it a creative venture. Some of these laws are or seem to be contradictory. For example, on the one hand you need to challenge the emptiness; on the other hand, you need to welcome it. This seems a contradiction, yet it is not. Both attitudes are necessary.

Another apparent contradiction is that it is extremely important for you to be receptive in an expectancy, yet this expectancy must be without preconceived ideas and without impatience and without wishful thinking. This seems very hard to explain in human words. It is something you have to feel into to be able to understand what I am saying to you here: there must be a positive expectancy which is yet free from specifics and preconceived notions of how and what should happen. There is another apparent contradiction in that you need to be specific, as I have often pointed out, yet this specificity must be light and neutral. You must be specific in one way, but not in another. If this seems confusing now, ask your inner being to relay the comprehension to your mind, rather than trying to understand with your mind.

The workings of the greater self so far surpass the mind's imagination and ability to conceive, that specificity would be a hindrance. Yet the mind must know what it wants, be prepared for it, reach for it and claim it, know that it deserves it and will not misuse it. The outer mind must make constant changes and readjustments in order to adapt itself to the greater scope of the inner God Consciousness. Your outer mind must become still and empty and receptive, yet it must hold itself poised for all possibilities. Thus it will be able to mate with the inner stillness, that appears first as emptiness. As you do this in a spirit of positive expectancy yet empty in mind and soul, patient and persevering, a new fullness and filling can take place. The inner stillness will begin to sing, as it were. From the energetic point of view it will convey light and warmth. Strength you never knew you possessed will arise. From the point of view of consciousness, knowledge, guidance, truth, inspiration, wisdom and advice will come for all your daily affairs, for your life in the biggest and smallest issues.

I have said this before, but it needs to be repeated. The process of receptive, creative emptiness must truly be nurtured. You must listen with an inner ear, and yet it is necessary that you do not pressure it but become receptive to when and how it will fill you. This is the only way, my friends, to find your inner sustenance, to find your divinity and to become a receptacle for the great universal power that is being released and that will manifest in your life, even more than a number of you have already experienced and increasingly experience.

This is a new important time in the history of evolution, and you are all needed to comprehend and perpetuate a renewal, a great change in thinking and perception, in the laws and the values, the great change that the Christ Consciousness is spreading. The way must be open from within and from without so as to make as many receptacles as possible.

The mind is an instrument that can be of hindrance or of aid to this process. You all know that your mind is limited only by your own concept of its limitations. To the degree you limit your mind you cannot perceive what is beyond the mind. The mind is finite and it must aim to spread the boundaries of its finiteness until it measures up with the infinite that is beyond the mind and that is within yourself, right here, right now. Then the mind merges into the infinite consciousness of your inner universe, in which you are one with all that is and yet all is infinitely personal.

As it is now, you carry your mind with you almost as a burden. It is a burden because it has become a closed circuit. Inside that circuit there is a certain leeway for the ideas, opinions, knowledge, concepts, possibilities that you have made room for in your life as a result of your education and the mores of your society. That circuit contains what you have chosen to learn and adopt as knowledge, both as part of the group consciousness and as your personal experience. To the degree you have grown and expanded, to that degree the closed circuit of your mind has widened. However, it is still a closed circuit. You are still burdened with ideas of limitation for yourself and your world. It is therefore necessary, in order to elicit and encourage creative emptiness, that you visualize the boundaries of your mind by questioning yourself about all the things that you think are impossible for you. Where you are hopeless and frightened there must be an idea of finiteness that is simply locked in your mind; thus you lock out the great power that is here for all those who are ready to receive it honestly.

Again we have an apparent contradiction. On the one hand, it is extremely necessary that this limited mind open itself up to other, new ideas and possibilities, as you have already learned to do in your own meditation. You have seen infallibly that where you have made room for a desirable new possibility, it indeed came into your life. You have also experienced that when it does not come into your life, then you deny that it can do so, for whatever reason. It is therefore necessary that you begin to puncture that closed circuit. You cannot immediately dissolve it. You live with a mind and you need your mind. It has functions in your life at this point, so what you need to do is puncture it. Where it is punctured, the flow of new energy and consciousness can penetrate. Where it is not punctured, you stay locked within the narrow confines of this limited mind that your spirit is fast outgrowing. On the other hand, as I have said, your mind must rest, not hold opinions, be neutral, in order to be a receptive vehicle for the great new force sweeping the inner universe of all consciousness.

But let us return to the process of puncturing the limited mind. How do you do this? As I said so often, you do this by first making it known to yourself that you do hold limited beliefs, instead of unquestioningly taking them for granted. The next step is to challenge them. This requires taking the trouble to walk through, in the well-practiced attitude of self-observation and self-confrontation, your limited beliefs and to truly think about them. Sometimes it is not just that you hold a false belief, but also that you have a stake in it; this must be examined. Once you put together the negative belief and the possible negative intentionality in holding on to it, you can see how you keep the circuit closed and deprive yourself of the inner replenishment you yearn for.

Another law of great importance for this purpose is that the opening to the greater universal consciousness must not be approached in a spirit of magic that is supposed to eliminate the becoming, the growing, and the learning process. Now, in whatever way this ultimate power is supposed to fill and sustain you, your outer mind must go through the steps of acquiring whatever knowledge and know-how are necessary. You all see this in the fields of arts and sciences. You cannot be inspired as a great artist, no matter how much genius you have, unless you learn the craft and the technical dexterity. If the childish lower self wants to use the channel to the greater universe in order to avoid the initial tedium of learning and becoming, the channel will remain closed. For this amounts to cheating, and God cannot be cheated. It is then that the personality may become seriously doubtful that anything beyond the mind exists, because no inspirational response comes forth when using "magic" to coddle the sense of laziness and self-indulgence. The same is true of science or any other field.

Now how about this same law in respect to inspiration for your personal life and decisions? Here, too, you must not fail to go through the work that the outer self has to do in order to become a proper channel for the God Consciousness. You do this in the pathwork. You need to truly know yourself, your pitfalls, your weaknesses, your lower self, where you are corruptible, where you are dishonest or tend to be. As you all know, this is hard work, but it needs to be done. If you avoid it, the channel will never really be reliable and may contain a lot of wishful thinking, stemming from man's "desire nature," or it may reveal "truth" that is based on guilt and fear and is thus equally unreliable. Only when you work in this fashion on your development will you come to a point when you no longer confuse gullibility and wishful thinking with faith, or doubt with discrimination. As the great pianist can only be a channel for higher inspiration when he goes through the finger exercises and hard and long practice that make his playing finally effortless, so must the God-inspired person work on his purification process, on deep self-knowledge and self-honesty. Only then does the receptacle becomes commensurate with higher truths and values and fit to be influenced, molded and used for higher purposes to enrich the world and the self.

At the same time you need to cultivate a neutrality. Your devotion to fulfilling the will of God needs to establish an attitude that whatever comes from God is all right, whether you desire it or do not desire it. Too much desire is as much a hindrance as the absence of all desire which manifests as resignation and hopelessness. The refusal to endure any kind of frustration creates an inner tension and defensive structure that close up the vessel of the mind and maintain the closed circuit. In other words, you, as a receptacle, need to be neutral. You need to give up the strong, tight, self-willed yes or no to make way for a flexible trust guided by your inner God. You need to be willing, pliable, flexible, trusting and forever ready for another turn, another change you had not contemplated. What is right now may not be right tomorrow.

There is no fixedness when it comes to the divine life that springs from within your innermost being. This idea makes you insecure, for you believe that security lies in fixed rules. Nothing could be further from the truth. This is one of those beliefs that need to be challenged. Envisage that in the idea of forever meeting every new situation by being inspired anew, in knowing that what is right in one situation may not be right in another, there lies a new security that you have not as yet found. This is one of those laws of the new age that is opposed to the old laws, according to which what is fixed, "stable," unmoving, unchangeable is supposedly secure.

The laws that pertain to this new venture into your inner creativity and life need to be studied very carefully; you must work with them. These are not just words to listen to, you need to make them your own. These laws are apparently full of contradiction. I say that you need to acquire knowledge and know-how, the mind must be widened and expanded, it must be able to conceive of truthful possibilities, and yet I say make your mind neutral and empty. This seems contradictory from the point of view of the dualistic consciousness, but from the point of view of the new consciousness that is spreading through your inner universe, these are not contradictions at all. For years I have tried to show you in many, many areas how this principle works: that something that is in truth and commensurate with the higher laws of life conciliates opposites that are mutually exclusive on the lower level of consciousness. What is conflict-producing on the lower level is mutually helpful and interactive on the higher level.

More and more you discover the truth of unification, where dualities cease to exist and contradictions are no longer contradictions, where you experience two previous opposites as two aspects of the same truth, both having their validity. When man begins to comprehend this principle and applies it to his own life, his outlook, his values, then indeed he is ready to receive the new consciousness released in realms far beyond his own.

When I say you must not approach the divine channel in you in an attitude that it should save you labor and work and the reality of living and growing, I am not saying it as a contradiction to the necessity of being passively receptive. It is simply a shift of the balance structure: where you were before over-active with your mind, you now need to quiet down and let happen; where you insisted on taking the controls, you must now relinquish control and let an inner, new power take over. On the other hand, where you tended before to be lazy and self-indulgent and looked for the line of least resistance and therefore made yourself dependent on others, you now need to take over and actively nurture the principles that establish the channels to your inner God. You also need to actively express its messages into life. So, as I said many years ago, activity and passivity need to be reversed.

Your mind will thus become an instrument. It will widen and open up and puncture its limitations and acquire new concepts, new considerations, with which your mind "plays around" for a while. It is the attitude of lightness in your perceptions, of flexibility, of motility of mind, that will make you the most receptive instrument, so that you can receive from your apparent emptiness.

Now, my friends, as we approach this emptiness, how does it feel? What is it all about? Again, the human language is extremely limited and it is almost impossible to squeeze experience such as this into the context of language. However, I will try my very best to give you some further helpful hints. As you listen into your inner "chasm," it seems at first to be a black chasm of emptiness. What you feel at this point is fear, and this fear seems to fill you up. What is this fear? It is as much a fear of finding yourself to be indeed empty, as of finding yourself with a new consciousness, with a new being evolving from within you. Although you yearn for this, you also fear it. The fear exists in both possibilities: you want the new consciousness so much that you fear the disappointment and yet you also fear finding it, for all the obligations and changes that this might impose upon you. You must travel through the fear—both these fears. On this path you have received the tools to deal with such fears by questioning your lower self.

But the time comes when you are ready, notwithstanding the still existing fear because, having made the connections, you have the knowledge of what your lower self wants, why you have negative intentionality. The time comes when, in spite of the fear, you decide calmly and quietly to go into the emptiness. So you make yourself empty in mind in order to meet the emptiness from deep within. Lo and behold, very soon that very emptiness will feel, not full in the same way you are used to, but the emptiness will contain a new aliveness that the old fullness made impossible. In fact, you will soon find out that you made yourself artificially full by packing yourself tight: tight in the mind with its noise, and tight within your channel by contracting your energy system into the hard knots of a defensive stance. You killed your aliveness with this fullness. So you became needier because without your inner life you cannot be fulfilled in a real sense. The vicious circle was established by striving to get it from outside of you, since you refused to go through the necessary steps to find it within.

In one sense you fear the aliveness more than the emptiness and perhaps you had better come face to face with that. When you make yourself sufficiently empty, the initial response is an inner aliveness, and you tend to immediately shut the lid tight again. Yet by denying that you fear the aliveness, you also deny that you are really very unhappy about the lack of aliveness. But aliveness is lacking because you fear it; through going into your fear of aliveness you will allow it to be as you let yourself be creatively empty. You will feel your whole being, including your body and your energetic inner being as if there were an "inner tube" that is alive, come vibrantly alive. Energy goes through it, feelings go through it, and something else comes to the fore which you cannot name as yet. If you do not shy away from that unnameable something, it will sooner or later turn out to be immanent instruction, constant inner ongoing instruction—truth, encouragement, wisdom, guidance, specifically destined for your life right now, wherever you need it most. That emptiness, that vibrant alive emptiness, is God talking to you. At any moment of the day it is talking to you where you need it most. If you really wish to hear it and attune to it, you will discern it, first vaguely, later strongly. You need to condition your inner ear to recognize it. As you begin to recognize the vibrant alive voice that speaks in wisdom and love—not in generalities, but specifically to you— you will know that this voice has always existed in you but you have conditioned yourself not to hear it. And in that conditioning you have tightened and packed up that "inner tube" that is to fill you with the vibrant music of the angels. When I say the "music of the angels," I do not necessarily mean this literally, although that too may occur. What you need is the instruction, the guidance, the help, in every thought, every decision about what opinion, what attitude to adopt in a given situation. That instruction is truly comparable to the music of the angels in its glory. This fullness cannot be described in its wonder, it is a treasure that is beyond all words. It is what you constantly look and yearn for, but most of the time you are not aware of this searching and project it onto substitute fulfillments that come from outside.

What you need to do is to refocus into what has always existed, and is now existing within you. Your mind and outer will have gone through such complicated procedures to confuse the issue and thus complicate your life that it is like finding your way out of a maze—a maze you have created. You can recreate your inner landscape without that maze.

Now, my dearest friends, at the end of this lecture I would like to say a few words about the new human being in the new era. What is the new man? What is the new woman? He or she is indeed always a receptacle of the Universal Intelligence, the Divine Consciousness, the Christ Consciousness that permeates every particle of being and of life. The new person does not function, decide, think habitually from the head and intellect. For many centuries the intellect had to be cultivated as a stepping stone on the evolutionary path, but the emphasis has now gone on too long. This does not mean that we should revert back to the purely blind, emotional "desire-nature"; it means that it is time to open up to a higher realm of consciousness within man and let this unfold. There was a period in evolution when it was as hard for man to find his ability to think, to weigh, to discriminate, to retain knowledge, to remember, in short, to use all the faculties of the mind, as it now seems hard to find contact with the higher self. The new human being has established a new balance in his inner system. The mind, the intellect must not be left out; it is a tool that must become unified with the greater consciousness. For many ages man believed that the faculties of the mind and intellect are the highest form of development. Some still believe this now, so they make no attempt to journey further and deeper into their inner nature, to find greater treasures. On the other hand, there are many spiritual movements which seek to discard and inactivate the mind altogether. This is equally undesirable because it creates a split rather than unification.

Both these extremes are half-truths, though they can have relative validity. For example, in the past men were like beasts, undisciplined and irresponsible as far as their immediate desires were concerned. They were totally driven by emotions and desires, regardless of concepts of ethics and morality. So for that stage, the development of the intellect fulfilled a restraining function as a sharp tool of learning, of discriminating. But when it ends there it becomes a farce; man becomes a farce when he cannot become animated by his divinity. By the same token, the practice of leaving the mind temporarily inactive is advisable, and I recommend it myself. But to accuse the mind as if it were the devil and to oust it from human life is missing the point.

In either extreme, man is not full, and he needs all his functions intact in order to express his divinity. Without a mind, he becomes a passive amoeba; when the mind is deemed the highest faculty, he becomes an overactive robot. The mind then becomes a computerized machine. True aliveness exists only when you wed the mind with the spirit and allow the mind to express the feminine principle for a while. All this time the mind has been engaged in the masculine principle—drive, action, control. Now the mind has to express the feminine principle—receptivity. This does not mean that man will become passive—by no means. In a different sense he will be more active, more truly independent that he was before. When the mind receives inspiration from the God Consciousness, it must be put into action. This putting into action is harmonious, effortless, not a cramp. When your mind is receptive, it can be filled with the higher spirit within you; then its functioning becomes totally different, forever new and exciting. Nothing becomes routine, nothing becomes stale, nothing becomes redundant, for the spirit is forever alive and changing. This is the energy and experience you have increasingly found at your Center, where the new influx is working so strongly.

The new person makes all his decisions from this other consciousness because he has worked his way through to be truly receptive to his own spiritual being. Thus the results in his life would sound utopian for someone who has not begun to experience this. I am so happy to say that quite a number of you are already part of this strong cosmic movement to which you have made yourselves available. You experience hitherto undreamed-of expansion and joy, resolutions of problems that you never thought possible—and it continues. There are no limitations to your fulfillment, to the peace, to the productivity, to the creativity of living, in every way and on every level; to joy, love, and happiness, and to the meaning your life has as you serve a greater cause. The time has passed when each individual can live only for his selfish, immediate little life. This can no longer be. Those who insist on this block out a power that would turn destructive in a mind that is still geared to selfishness. That selfishness comes from the false belief that you are happy only when you are selfish and unhappy when you are unselfish. That false belief is one of the first myths you need to explore and challenge.

You create a new life for yourself and your environment, of a kind that mankind has not yet known. You are preparing for it, others are preparing for it here and there, all over the world, quietly. These are golden nuclei that spring up out of the grey and dark matter of untruthful thinking and living. Further that channel in you. It is the excitement and the peace you have always wanted. Enter this new phase, my dearest friends, with courage and affirmation. Get out of the attitude toward yourself in which you feel beaten down. You are not beaten down, unless you affect this role. You can become who you truly are and experience life at its best.

All of you are blessed, my very dearest ones. The blessings will give you the sustenance you need to go all the way with all of yourself and become enlivened, activated, actualized by the God within. Be in peace.

Glossary

The Higher Self, The Lower Self, And The Mask

In an effort to represent human nature in its completeness, we can conceive of it in the shape of three concentric spheres. The outer sphere we call the mask self. This we fashion according to how we want others to see us, and how we would like to believe we are. The mask self is also a protection against what we don't want others to see and what we don't want to see within ourselves. In the sense that we want to impress others with it, the mask self is an aspect of what we call the "ego." It is a controlled and manipulated expression of ourselves, created for the purpose of attaining some of our hidden and partly unconscious goals.

In creating his mask self, man works—of course mostly unconsciously—like a sculptor with a model. The model which we try to copy when we make our mask is the idealized self-image. It is a conception of what we want to be, not in the deeply satisfying spiritual sense, but in the sense of meeting the expectations of others and of trying to escape from our own fears. Thus, the idealized self-image contains many harmful misconceptions of which we are unaware. Nevertheless, it has a strongly negative power and controls our lives through the mask self.

Behind the mask self hides the second sphere, that hidden world of egocentricity which we call the lower self. This is actually what the mask self covers up, because we do not want to display or face the fear, the hate, the stinginess, the cruelty, the distorted perceptions, and the intellectual misconceptions of the lower self. It is in the lower self that images have their seat and give rise to negative reactions and patterns which create conflict and misery in our lives.

Contrary to many modern, pessimistic appraisals of human nature, which identify man with his lower self, man has a higher self, which is the inmost core of his nature. This higher self is part of the universal intelligence and universal love that pervades all life, in short, of God. It is our divine spark. This higher self is free, spontaneous, loving, giving, all-knowing, and capable of uninterrupted joy and bliss. It is the brief contacts with this higher self that give man his true happiness, his creativity, and his real pleasure. We can get in touch with our higher self through being in truth, giving from our heart and not for personal gain or reward, through caring for and loving each other, and through meditation and prayer.

Images

Man is not born with a clear, undistorted perception of reality. Due to his previous incarnations and the circumstances of his childhood in this life, he sees many situations in a distorted way. When these distortions develop into a firmly-held conclusion about life, we speak of an image. An image is made up of misconceptions, distorted feelings, and physical blocks. Of course, a conclusion drawn from distorted perception is a wrong conclusion; therefore images are actually wrong conclusions about the nature of reality which are so firmly embedded in a person's psyche that they become behavior-controlling signals in life situations. An image of this kind is not subjected to rational examination, but is often defended by elaborate rationalizations. A person may have several images, but underlying them all is a main image, which is the key to his basic negative attitude toward life.

An example of an image formed under childhood conditioning might be that the display of emotion, especially of warm feelings, is a sign of weakness and will lead to one's being hurt. Although this is a personal image, it may be reinforced by the societal mass image that, especially for a man, the display and physical expression of warm feelings is unmanly and weak because it means losing control. An individual with this image will then, in any situation where he could emotionally open himself, obey the signal of the images instead of spontaneously responding to the actual situation or person, which would be the positive, life-affirming response. He also acts toward others in such a way that they will respond negatively to him and confirm his false belief. Thus he deprives himself of pleasure and restricts the flow of the life force, creating inner tensions and further feeding his image. The effect of such images on the individual is the creating of negative compulsive patterns and reactions that restrict the unfolding of his potential.

Vicious Circle

Psychologically speaking, a vicious circle is a self-perpetuating, repetitive pattern of negative, destructive, illusory attitudes which intensify one another. It originates in an image or misconception which separates us from the reality of a situation; as the vicious circle progresses, we get further and further away from correcting the original mistake. Take, for instance, somebody who has the misconception that the only way to defend himself against being hurt by others is to make them afraid of him. Even if he initially did not elicit hostile feelings, in his endeavor to frighten others he will certainly evoke them. This hostility will make him more threatening and tyrannical and he will use all new evidence to reconfirm his original misconception. Finally he is bound to have some unpleasant experience, which he will interpret as the result of his not having been "strong enough." Thus he remains a prisoner of his vicious circle and goes through the same experience again and again.

The vicious circle may be broken only when the man finds the point where he is able to abandon one of the wrong attitudes which make up the circle. Once this attitude is given up, one can begin to see the situation more realistically and begin to question the basic misconception in order to create a truly benign circle.

Duality

Human beings live in duality. Thus they perceive everything through pairs of opposites: good or evil, light or dark, right or wrong, living or dead. This is so because our consciousness is split. This dualistic way of perceiving conceals from us the deeper reality of the universe, which is fundamental unity. Every soul longs for the unified state of consciousness—a state of absolute reality, bliss, freedom, and fulfillment. It is possible to attain, or at least catch glimpses of this state, for our real self lives in this unified state even when we are unaware of it. We experience it when we identify with our higher selves; then duality is transcended. Once a soul has consciously experienced this state of being even for a second, there is always the possibility to challenge the split dualistic state by remembering one's true nature and the oneness of all life.

The Life Force

The Life Force is the free-flowing energy current manifest in the universe in all beings, things, and ideas. Nothing exists without it. The life force has three essential aspects: movement, consciousness, and experience.

When we do not resist the life force which is always flowing through us, we can experience utter bliss. This becomes possible when our entire organism is in harmony with reality on the physical, emotional, mental, and spiritual levels. This means giving up misconceptions and defenses which prevent integration of the personality with the life force. To make this possible we must be in movement, allow ourselves to grow, attain a consciousness beyond duality, and experience all feelings deeply without resistance.

Even in our present state of being we can contact the life force when we clarify the confusion of distorted feelings, thoughts, and moods. When we accept the truth of the present state and are willing to be in the now, we will immediately become imbued with the wisdom and joy of the life force. As our development continues, the life force is experienced not only in rare moments, but becomes a part of our life: we become fully one with the life force.

Christ Consciousness

The Christ Consciousness is an awareness of a divine energy influx manifesting as an evolutionary force within all Creation and therefore within each human being. This consciousness transcends any specific belief, spiritual practice, or religion.

The Christ Consciousness infuses the New Age—the age of communication—on three levels.

The first level is man's connection to God. Jesus Christ embodied this when He said, "I and the Father are one." In such a state of being we know that we can use every experience as a stepping stone to greater revelation; we have a greater willingness to release our human will to the divine will. Each one of us can draw on this ocean of unlimited power and love, of new life and new light, just as we draw every breath we take into our body.

The second level is man's relationship to man. Here the Christ Consciousness manifests as a powerful force sweeping the earth to bring about world-wide caring among races, nations, and individuals. It is the consciousness that all people are brothers and sisters inhabiting the same home, the planet earth.

The third level is man's relationship to the natural world, to the reality of the earth as a living being needing care and sensitivity. The beauty and productivity of the earth, the creatures of land and sea are the responsibility of the newly-awakened man and woman of the New Age who are expressing the Christ Consciousness.

The Christ Consciousness radiates unconditional love and universal brotherhood.

List of Available Guide Lectures*

1. The Sea of Life
2. Decisions and Tests
3. Choosing Your Destiny
4. World Weariness
5. Happiness as a Link in the Chain of Life
7. Asking for Help and Helping Others
9. The Lord's Prayer
11. Know Yourself
13. Positive Thinking
14. The Higher Self, the Lower Self, and the Mask
15. Influence between the Spiritual and Material Worlds
16. Spiritual Nourishment
17. The Call
18. Free Will
19. Jesus Christ
20. God—the Creation
21. The Fall
22. Salvation
25. The Path
26. Finding One's Faults
27. Escape Possible Also on the Path
28. Communication with God
29. Activity and Passivity
30. Self-Will, Pride, and Fear
31. Shame
32. Decision-Making
33. Occupation with Self
34. Preparation for Reincarnation

* The numbers and titles omitted in this list were Question and Answer Sessions given to those present at the meeting.

These lectures are available for $2.00 each from:
> The New York Pathwork Office
> 36 East 20th Street
> New York, NY 10003
>> Telephone: (212) 505-0230
>> *and*
> The Phoenicia Pathwork Center
> P.O. Box 66
> Phoenicia, NY 12464
>> Telephone: (914) 688-2211
>> *also:*
> The Sevenoaks Pathwork Center
> Route 1, Box 86
> Madison, VA 22727
>> Telephone: (703) 948-6544

"Be blessed, every one of you.

Those of you who want to make a commitment to your inner being and avail yourselves of the help this particular path can give are blessed and guided in all your efforts.

And those who do not wish to take this step yet, or are drawn elsewhere, they too are being blessed.

Be in peace."

—The Guide

The Pathwork

The lectures are the foundation of the Pathwork, a contemporary spiritual discipline. People from all over the world have been attracted to these teachings and through reading and discussing the lectures in an informal setting, spiritual communities have sprung up in New York City; Detroit, Michigan; Boston, Massachusetts; Washington, D.C.; Iowa; Holland; Germany, Italy and Venezuela. People study the lectures, work with a helper, participate in groups and take intensive retreats, according to their interest and degree of involvement. There are also two residential Pathwork communities, where people experiment with and explore what it means to live in community. One is in Phoenicia, New York; the other in Madison, Virginia.

We welcome your inquiries and honor your search. For further information, please call or write: The Phoenicia Pathwork Center, Box 66, Phoenicia, New York 12464; (914) 688-2212.